I0169471

Growing Up

on the Farm

1937-1960

Michael J. Danehy

Edited by Patricia Danehy Catsos and
Christine Elizabeth Catsos

©2014 Michael J. Danehy

Pond Cove Press

PO Box 10106

Portland, ME 04104

ISBN: 978-0-9916019-0-5

All rights reserved. No part of this publication may be reproduced, stored in a retrieval system or transmitted, in any form or by any means, electronic, mechanical, photocopying, recording, or otherwise, without prior written permission of the author.

Table of Contents

Introduction

The farm, circa 1950.

I, Mike Danehy, was born on August 28, 1937, in Canastota, NY. My Dad ran a farm which was owned by my Grandfather Danehy. The farm was 200 acres, about 110 tillable, and supported about sixty milk cows. It was good land, and life was good there when I was young. The farm was in Madison County, NY, looking out over the Mohawk Valley to the North. You could see all of Oneida Lake from the barn door, and the lights of Syracuse and Utica lit up the sky to the West and the East at night.

My whole life growing up revolved around the farm, the neighbors, my parents, our relatives, my brother Jim, my sisters Patsy and Mary Ellen, and especially my brother Bill, who was only twelve months older than me. Bill and I spent a great deal of time together, and it is a miracle we didn't kill each other, as we often disagreed on the approach to be taken in solving the many problems we faced, some of which were about play, some about work, and some about nothing at all. I am happy to say that now, in 2014, we are still friends, and can laugh at most of the old conflicts.

My first real memories were when I was about t h r e e years old. I remember being able to look up over the rim of the sink. I thought what a big boy I was! This is also about the time I started being a little hell raiser, along with brother Bill.

Mike at 3 years, outside the "old" porch.

We lived two miles from Perryville, NY, a miserable little town of about 250 people, sunk down in a hollow, and inhabited by some pretty poor souls, even though the farms in the surrounding country were quite prosperous. I went to school in Perryville for the first 5 years, in a one room schoolhouse. More later on that. Let me tell you first about Ma and Dad, the neighbors and some of Dad's relatives who lived near the farm.

My Dad and His Buddies

Dad and Lassie, circa 1950.

My father, Francis William "Buster" Danehy, was a very good man who had good times and bad times, mostly good. The worst time was when Grandpa died and didn't leave a will, presenting a great problem to my parents, left with five kids and a future which looked bleak at the time. But they got by that, and that experience was a good lesson for us kids, though it took a toll on both Mom and Dad. More to come on this topic later on. Dad was quite a hell-raiser and man about town in his youth. He and others tried to put a wagon up on the roof of the school one Halloween. I don't know if they succeeded, but some adults chased them, and Dad fell and broke his leg trying to escape. Another time he didn't want to go to school, so he rubbed leeks all over himself, until he smelled so bad they kicked him out of school for the day.

Dad rode the milk train to high school every day, riding from Perryville to Canastota. One day, someone on the train gave him a bag full of B-Bs, which he carried into the three story school building. The hot air heating system had vents in each room, and sheet metal ducts from floor to floor.. He and a few friends thought it would be good to throw B-Bs down the vents, which they did, to much accompanying clatter. It was fun, but he got caught, and it was no fun staying after school and picking up BBs for the next few days!

We think he was quite a lady's man at one time. I know Bill and I had a lot of fun reading the love letters he saved in a drawer in one of the rooms upstairs. He started college in Engineering at Syracuse University, but between girls and parties, he didn't last long. He eventually got serious and was doing well in school at Kansas City Aeronautical Institute until Grandpa got sick and Dad had to come home and run the farm.

Dad was a fine neighbor. He was always helping the neighbors do something with their houses, when we needed the same thing done at our house. Ma used to get pretty mad at him for doing their work instead of ours. Dad was good at figures, and did the taxes for everybody in the neighborhood.

Dad and Ma were always taking in stray people. Thumper Rouse stayed at our house off and on for years, as did a kid named "Red." Uncle Matt Baker was there at times, until he would get mad and leave. When we were young, Jerry Foley, Dad's nephew, lived with us, as did a girl named Doris Melansen, and another young man named Bernard. Also in the house were Grandpa and Grandma Danehy. Most of these people worked on the farm while with us, but you can see that it was a busy place with a lot of mouths to feed, and this didn't count all the Ryan and Martin visitors!

Well, there were some bad times at the farm, usually a result of Dad and his friends drinking more than they should have, or the lack of money, or the fact that Dad didn't really like farming, or all of the above.

I remember once when Dad couldn't pay the bill for the propane tank we used to run the kitchen gas stove and water heater. The gas company sent Dad a letter saying if he didn't pay, they were going to come and shut off the gas. He was very angry. He called them on the phone and told them to come and get their gas tank and controls, and if they and their equipment weren't off our property in one hour, they would find their equipment thrown in the middle of the road. I think they gave him added time to pay the bill.

Dad used to take us fishing quite often. This is one of my fondest memories with him. Over time, we fished most streams in Madison County, and he took me to the headwaters of every stream which originated in the county. There was a divide running through Madison County, with streams north of the divide flowing to the St. Lawrence River, and those south of the divide flowing eventually to the Chesapeake Bay. I was very interested in this and once gave a speech with maps to the English class in eighth grade. But these trips would often wind up with us in trouble, as he would stop in one or more of his favorite bars on the way home, and when we got home, he would get a tongue lashing from Ma, and wind up milking late.

I'm afraid Ma put up with a lot of this sort of thing through those hard times. I can remember going to town for groceries with the whole family, and after shopping, he would stop at Lynch's in Cazenovia and have a beer or two while we, including Ma, sat in the car waiting. I don't think that marriage would have survived in today's social environment, and later on Ma put her foot down on that kind of thing.

Dad had a lot of favorite bars, and a lot of friends who frequented each of them. He liked Lynch's in Cazenovia, The Cazenovia House, Slabsides in Erieville, The Ten Pin in Chittenango, Nelson Inn in Nelson, and several bars in Canastota, which he used to visit with Uncle Charlie Pickard and with Tucker. By the way, all these bars are long gone. Maybe people don't drink as much now as they did then.

Some of his friends had real drinking problems. Joe Ryan used to go on "benders," when he would get drunk and disappear for days. Mike Driscoll ran a gas station in Cazenovia. We used to sit in the station with him and shoot the breeze. Then he and Dad would go over to Lynch's for a few beers. Mike liked to fight when he got drinking. He once got in a huge fight at Lynch's and broke up most of the furniture. I once asked my Dad if he ever got in a fight. He said no, and when I asked him why not, he said, "because it takes a hell of a mad man to catch a scared one."

One of Dad's buddies was Zeke Emhof, another unmotivated farmer, but a real nice guy. Someone once asked Zeke when he milked his cows. His answer was, "I milk in the morning when I get up, and at night when I get home!" Another time, Zeke and another guy, Pete, were hunting for a bull which had gotten loose and gone wild. It was winter, and they were hunting with rifles, and wearing snowshoes. They eventually came upon the bull, and as they started to fire, the bull charged them. Pete was blasting away, but the bull kept coming, and Zeke was bent over taking off his snow shoes. Pete said, "what in hell are you doing?" Zeke said, "I would look funny climbing that tree over there with these snow shoes on, wouldn't I?" Well, they got the bull in the end, but I guess Pete wasn't too happy with Zeke. Another time, Zeke was out drinking late, and he finally said, "well, I better get home to hold the flashlight for Margaret," (his long suffering wife). "She hates to climb up in the silo and throw down ensilage in the dark."

One year I came home from college for the summer, hoping for a construction job. Dad told me Zeke had a job for me the next day. (By this time Zeke had quit farming and was working construction). Next day we went to Syracuse where they were building a bridge, and I shoveled concrete from about 6:30 AM until 7:00 PM. I was so tired I could hardly stand up and barely talk, but Zeke, who had an easier job all day, was driving, and he thought it would be good to have a few drinks on the way home. Now at that time, I enjoyed a few beers myself, but not when I was so tired I couldn't hold up a beer glass. We got home about 10:00 PM, and went right back to work the next day. I worked most of that summer with Zeke. He got me an easy job on a road construction crew. He and I got the job of coating freshly poured concrete with a tar mixture used to slow down the rate at which the concrete cured, a much more civilized job than shoveling concrete all day. We only had one problem. One day the hose ruptured, and high pressure tar sprayed all over Zeke. We called him tar baby after that. He was a sight to see.

Dad supervising at camp, circa 1975.

Another one of Dad's buddies was Jiggs Ryan, a car dealer and cousin of Ma's. Jiggs liked to play cards, and so did Dad except Dad had no money. More than once I saw Jiggs slip Dad a few bucks to stay in a game at the Cazenovia House. One evening, Jiggs came home with Dad to lend moral support after they had been out all afternoon. Ma accused Dad of having too much to drink. Jiggs stepped in and said, "Now, now, Anna, he is well preserved, well preserved." Ma said, "Well preserved, he's pickled!" Well, Dad and Jiggs went to the barn to milk the cows. I remember Jiggs helping Dad milk in his three piece suit.

Dad used to like to go to the Ten Pin in Chittenango. Among his friends there was a guy who bought a new car, and bored everyone with details of what good mileage it got. One day when he wasn't there, they decided to play a trick on him. When he pulled in they would take turns adding several gallons of gas to his car without his knowledge. His mileage got better and better and he bragged more and more. After a few weeks, they stopped gassing him up, and his mileage went way down. It took him a long time to realize he had been the victim of a pretty good practical joke.

Ma and Dad at camp, circa 1980.

Dad had a lot of sayings that he liked to repeat on appropriate occasions. His favorite all time job was being a lock tender on the Barge Canal on the night shift. There was very little night traffic, and he took a chaise lounge with him in the truck every night, and slept most of the time. When a boat would come, the guy at the next lock up would call him, and he would jump up and open the lock. He would then get home about 8:00 AM and would come into the house or camp shouting, "there is a forenoon, you know. Everybody up!!" Or he would say, "is the Queen Bee up yet?" He also took a fish-pole every night, and in the winter took old furniture that needed refinishing.

Later on, they made him responsible for two or three locks due to lack of funds and lack of business, and that didn't make him too happy, though he still liked the job. When he was over 70, people started asking him when he would retire, and he always laughed and told them he retired on the day he sold the farm.

When Ma had a big gang to prepare a meal for, he would sit in his chair and say, "relax, Anna, relax." She was never too pleased to hear this. When Ma was bent over the sink or tending flowers, he would look at her rather impressive rear end and say, "Forty acres, and it's all mine." She pretty much just ignored this remark.

Dad loved butter, and used to eat it by the spoonful out of the large containers we bought at the milk plant. He said it was good for you, and insisted that Chinese people had slanted eyes because they didn't eat any butter. He didn't swear much, but when he was exasperated with us, he would say "by the Judas priest..." He had his own way of pronouncing some words. For instance, Miami was Meeami. Another saying was "They'll grow up de spite yah," used whenever any of us were critical of our own or other siblings' children. We never knew if he meant they will grow up in spite of you, or did he mean they will grow up to spite you.

On the day when Dad and Ma moved to Chittenango, in 1967 or '68, they drove separate cars and agreed to meet at the new house. Dad, however, made the mistake of stopping at the Ten Pin for a beer and to say hello to his friends. Ma waited for him to arrive, but knew very well where he was. She got in the car, went down there, and gave him a royal chewing out in front of his friends. That was the end to his bar visits without prior approval or Ma by his side. They lived happily ever after.

It seems like too much of the above narrative deals with Dad's misbehavior, but he furnished us with a good place to live, lots of good food, and between the two of them, an idea that we were pretty damn important people, and with hard work we could better ourselves and lead satisfying lives as adults. They never said we had to go to college, but it was really a given from the start. He went through some really hard times, but was usually upbeat, and really enjoyed life, especially after they bought the camp in Erieville.

Ma and Dad, 1983.

Ma

Ma, Anna Ryan Danehy, was a really great person. I don't think I appreciated what a terrific individual she was for a long, long time. I certainly loved her, but I don't think I felt the respect for her which she deserved until both she and I were much older. Late in her life, I finally realized what a strong woman she was, and how much leadership she brought to the family. Dad was the major provider, and the nominal head of the family, but Ma was the one who always kept us kids going in the right direction.

I think all of us felt we were her favorite, which is a fine parenting trick if you can do it. However, in reality I think I was really her favorite. I have some proof of this. For instance, she used to cut my corn off the cob for me, since I didn't like holding the ears. She didn't do that for the others. She was very sympathetic to my school bus headaches, and served me

Ma, in her usual spot, peeling potatoes.

breakfast on the couch, and didn't appear suspicious when the headaches disappeared when the school bus disappeared. When Dugan refused to get on the bus, she called Dad up from the barn to kick his fanny out to the road. See, I was favored.

Ma was a good cook, especially for a bunch of hungry farmers. Her coffee was a specialty. She had a large pot, which she filled with water, threw in a bunch of coffee grounds, and boiled the hell out of it until it was ready to turn to syrup. I started drinking that stuff when I was about five.

Her strong suit was to put on good meals for an unknown, but large, number of people with what seemed to be a minimum of effort, or at least a minimum of worry. She stayed good at that until near the end. Five

A crowd at the Danehy's, circa 1961.

o'clock would come; five, ten, or fifteen people would be sitting around, and she would say, "Well, what shall we have for supper?" and soon, as if by magic, a meal would appear, though a quick trip to the store was sometimes necessary.

We kids liked to sleep on the big open side porch in the summer, especially when the Martins were visiting. We didn't have sleeping bags, so Ma would drag our mattresses and blankets down from the bedrooms so we could sleep in comfort. The porch was heavily used during the day, so she would pick up all the bedding each day, and take it back in the house. Why would she do all that extra work, and why didn't we help her?

She was a pretty good nurse, and a good judge of major injuries requiring a trip to the doctor. I think the rule was if the bleeding stopped inside of an hour, and if no bones were sticking out, then no doctor. I remember trips to the doctor for broken arms, facial burns, boils, which were staph infections, and which I got regularly, but not for much else. Ma was primarily in charge of discipline, although she was quick to call on Dad if necessary. She didn't hit us often, but she did spank Bill and me with a razor strap once when we disobeyed her orders to stay on our own land.

When we went to college, Ma went back to work teaching in Chittenango. She loved that job, and she was good at it. From then on we called her "Ma the bank," since she paid most of the college bills. They used to give her many of the tough kids at school, primarily because of what most of her grandchildren called the "grandma grip." She would grab the misbehaving student by the upper arm, twist and raise the arm at the same time, and the student would be standing on his tippy toes, almost off the floor, and without exception became very cooperative. I suppose she would be sued and fired today, but it worked well at the time. Our other name for Ma, when she was older and less mobile, was "the dispatcher." She was in charge of knowing where everybody was at all times. If any of us wanted to know where any family member was, we just called the dispatcher. I notice in the hurricane disaster plans they want everyone here in Eastern Virginia to have, they suggest that some family member be designated as a source who knows where everyone is. That would be Ma.

Ma wasn't always treated well by Dad's relatives. She was pretty sensitive, and was hurt by comments like "who invited the Danehys?" Her relationship with Grandma Danehy was often a little strained. Grandma liked to be boss, and that only went just so far with Ma. Aunt Mary could also be nasty at times. She once told Ma that she raised five spoiled brats, which may have been true, but Ma didn't need to hear that from Aunt Mary.

I can remember some very hard times for Mom, after they had to sell the cows. Dad worked a number of temporary jobs, and either worked late or stopped after work to see his buddies. She would stand in the window, chewing her finger nails and sometimes crying, looking for his car to come down over the hill. Those times were very tough on the marriage, and she deserved a lot of credit for holding the family together. I think overall the marriage was well worth it to both of them, because they really did love one another, but it was tough and would not have weathered the storm today.

Today when you read about someone whose mother died when she was twelve, leaving six kids and a father with no money and poor job prospects, you look for the rest of the story to be a disaster. It didn't happen that way with Ma and her siblings. She grew up to be a teacher, a great Mom, and a person with an optimistic view toward the future for herself and all those around her. She was a great role model for all of us, and though she never said it in so many words, she expected us to do our best and to make something of ourselves in this world. I think all of us still reach for the telephone when we have a question about history, geography, food, or life in general. Too bad she didn't leave her new number.

The Neighbors

Smith Tucker- Tucker lived next door, about a quarter mile away. He farmed "on shares" meaning he didn't own the land. My Uncle Charlie Pickard owned it, but Tucker lived there and they shared the costs and income from the farm. Tucker was married to Glady, who was a darn good cook. Tucker was a gentle giant. He weighed about 230 pounds and was very strong. He usually wore bib overalls and a work shirt, and he chewed Redman tobacco. Lots of days he had a stubble of beard, and his teeth and stubble sometimes showed signs of tobacco juice. He usually did the dirty work on tough jobs, like butchering. When he whacked a cow with a sledge, down she went!

Tucker swore. Not just now and then, but in a steady stream. I can safely say that Tucker was responsible for getting me out of going to church for several years because of the words he taught me. Once he and a hired man sat me down and taught me how to say "son-a-bitch" and other similar adjectives. Ma was very pleased. One time Tucker and my Dad were leaning on the pickup truck visiting, when the priest came by to see my Grandmother. Father joined the group leaning on the truck and listened to Tucker JC, GD, and SOB his way through some story. Then Tucker had to go. There was a short silence, then the priest said, "well, he wasn't swearing. It was just his manner of speaking."

Don't get me wrong. Tucker was the nicest man in the neighborhood in a lot of ways. He hauled us all over in the back of his truck. Picture five to ten kids and a dog or two going here and there. Seat belts? Forget it. He was a hard worker, and always there if my mother needed anything if Dad was away. Tucker knew right from wrong. The farmers used to get together to harvest the oat crop. One time when they were at our house, Ma cooked up a big noon meal for the crew, probably ten or twelve people. For dessert she served pie, which though tasty, had a rather tough crust. Now Tucker had a scrawny teenager named

Frankie Hill working for him at the time. He was sitting across the table from Tucker, when he said to my mother, "can I have another piece of that rubber pie?" Some people started to laugh, but Tucker stood up, reached across the table, snatched Frankie Hill by the shirt, yanked him over the table, out into the yard, and gave him a good thrashing. Nothing more was said, but I'd guess Frankie never asked for rubber pie again. Tucker was a big part of our everyday lives, and you will hear more of him as time goes by.

Leighton Smith- He was a minor character in the neighborhood. Dave Ingram, who was our great friend, lived with Leighton, and with his wife, Aunt Jessie. Aunt Jessie used to be our babysitter, God bless her. Also living with the Smiths were Dave's sisters, the three Ingram girls, Pat, Wilma, and Mary. They were older than us, and the subject of some fantasies on our part.

The only thing I remember about Leighton was the way he drove his car. He was quite an old man, and a car was a challenge to him. On rare occasions, we would ride with him, 3 or 4 of us in the back seat. He drove about ten or fifteen miles per hour max, but what we really loved about his driving was that he would blow his horn every time he went up a hill. He was hard of hearing, so wouldn't notice us howling with laughter in the back seat every time he went up a hill!

Claude Rouse- Claude was Uncle Charlie Pickard's hired man. He lived with his wife and kids in a tenant house on the Pickard farm. He was a real good guy, a hard worker, and like Tucker, a good friend to our family. Claude did love to drink a beer, smoke a cigarette, and tease anyone who looked vulnerable to it. He usually hadn't shaved in two or three days and had a cigarette hanging out of his mouth.

I learned one of life's little lessons from Claude one day when Dad and I went over to Uncle Charlie's for a visit. It was snowing nice wet snow perfect for snowballs. We were standing in the yard between the house and the barn, when Claude came out of the barn with a pail in each hand. I thought, "now there is a nice target for a snowball. He won't get me back because my Dad is here, and besides, he's only a hired man." Claude saw me looking and said, "don't throw that snowball at me." I threw it anyway and hit him. Maybe you can guess the rest. He put down the pails, grabbed me, kicked my butt once or twice, and washed my face in the snow. Dad and Uncle Charlie laughed, went on with their conversation, and paid no more attention to me. Lesson learned.

Two other quick stories about Claude. Once we were filling a silo and Claude had the miserable job of spreading the ensilage around in the silo after it was blown in by the ensilage cutter.

Between loads we were supposed to keep the ensilage cutter going to blow fresh air into the silo, as ensilage gives off gases which are poisononous, or at least replace the oxygen in the silo. Anyway, the machine got shut down, and Claude quickly started to feel the effects of the lack of air. He was able to shout that he was in trouble, air was quickly blown back in, and he was fine. But farming is dangerous, and serious accidents are always a possibility. The other story is about Claude's ability to consume beer. Dad was building a corn crib, and wanted a concrete floor. Forget Ready-Mix delivery. It all had to be mixed by hand. Claude said he would help if Dad would furnish the beer. They worked all day, with us kids watching in awe as Claude drank the case of beer (with a little help from Dad). That concrete floor, reinforced with 24 beer bottles, is still there.

Roland Younglove and his wife Imogene- I include them because Rollie always worked with us on threshing and corn harvesting, along with Tucker and Uncle Charlie. Also, he loved nicknames. He is the one who named brother James "Dugan." He used to call me Michalo-Angelo-Pete. Glad that didn't stick. Finally, he used to love it if Bill and I got in a fight when we were all working together. It made his day, and we often obliged.

Charlie Pickard and Aunt Sue- Uncle Charlie and Aunt Sue lived about a mile to the East of us. We saw a lot of them and their kids (Marianne, Rosie, and Chuckie). Uncle Charlie was the best farmer in the neighborhood. Chuck is still farming most of the same land, although he lives where Tucker used to live. Uncle Charlie was a very nice man. He was generous with us. He hauled the milk to Canastota to the Queensboro plant every day, and once in a while took one of us with him. We could always count on a stop at Fazio's or The Weaver for a beer afterward (beer for him, soda for us). Uncle Charlie had a good sense of humor and loved to laugh. After I started dating Sue, Aunt Sue invited everyone to dinner one evening. Aunt Sue hollered at Uncle Charlie, "Why don't you shave?" He said, "My beard wouldn't be so long if dinner was on time."

Stanley Pickard and his wife Adeline- Stanley was Jimmy "Pick" Pickard's Father, and a poor farmer if ever there was one. He was as bad at farming as Uncle Charlie Pickard was good. Their cows were constantly getting out because Stanley was too lazy to fix fence. One evening Bill and I were all dressed for town when we saw Stanley's cows in our corn. We rushed over to the field and chased the cows but were not having much luck. I shouted to Ma, "tell that son of a b---- Stanley to get up here and get these cows." At the same time, I had a large rock in both hands, a cow came charging down the next row over, and I let her have it right between the eyes. I looked up and there was Stanley. He said nothing and I said nothing, but he got the point. Another time, Stanley's electric fencer broke down. The fencer reduced the voltage on the fence so it would shock a cow but not hurt them. Stanley proceeded to hook his fence up directly to the 110 volt lines, which worked fine until some cows touched it and were electrocuted. At least it wasn't us kids. They lived next door to us on the West side, just a short distance away. Pick and I could get each others attention by shouting. Much more on Pick and some on Stanley later on. Stanley and Adeline had the first TV in the neighborhood. I think they had a TV when they were still going to the bathroom in a two-holer outhouse in their woodshed. Obviously, they had their priorities straight. Before that, I only saw TV when Dad took me to Lynch's bar in Cazenovia. I think the only things on were Howdy Doody,

Milton Berle, boxing and wrestling (which were on every night), and test pattern. Bill and I suddenly found excuses to be down at Stanley Pickard's every evening. It embarrassed my Grandmother so much that she finally bought us a set.

Ma and Pa Keville (pronounced Kiv-il)- They were Adeline's parents, and lived in the same house. Ma Keville was a tough, strong old lady, and you didn't cross her if you were smart. One time we were playing on their front porch. There was a clothesline tied to a corner post and over to a tree. She told us not to swing on the line, but as soon as she went in the house I gave it a try. The added weight yanked the post out from under the corner of the porch roof, and the roof partially fell down. (The house was not particularly well built.) Ma Keville was cutting cabbage with a butcher knife. She came charging out of the house and spanked me with the flat side of the butcher knife, and sent me home a running. I didn't tell Ma because I didn't want another whipping for the same sin!

The Manwarrens, Eddie and Eva- The Manwarrens lived down the road, across from Pick. When we were about 8 or 9 years old, Me and Bill and Pick and Dave got in the habit of walking down to their house, knocking on the door, and asking, "do you have any cookies today?" The answer was always yes, and we went away full. Eventually, my Mother found out what we were doing, and told us to stop being so rude. We did stop, and from then on, we would walk right on by Eva's house. She would often be pounding on the front room window, inviting us to stop, but we never did after that. I wonder what she thought happened! This is one of the only times I remember when Mom's judgment was wrong.

The Dougherty family- Bill and Kelly Dougherty and their kids, lived about two miles away, and were great friends of all us Danehys. Bill was another mediocre farmer, who was always a day late and a dollar short. He is one of the people we always wound up helping with work after we finished our own.

Dad would drag us up there to help, much against our wishes.

Kelly and Bill always treated us well, but his fields were full of holes and his equipment poor or nonexistent, so we would take our equipment and proceed to ruin it up there. Some fields were so bad, full loads of hay would tip over in the woodchuck holes or ditches. Frustrating work. Once, Bill borrowed my father's hydraulic jack, a big heavy one. He managed to run it through his ensilage cutter, which damaged the jack and totaled the ensilage cutter. I babysat for the Dougherty kids off and on. My requirements for sitting were that the family had to have a daughter old enough to change the other kid's diapers and bring me ice cream or other snacks. My role was primarily security and rule enforcement. I don't know why they hired me, because I would fall asleep and they couldn't wake me up when they got home, so I usually stayed all night. I remember sitting in the Dougherty kitchen in the morning, watching Bill and Kelly drink coffee and smoke cigarettes. They were always very interested in me and in what my plans were for the future. Sadly, the cigarettes caught up with both of them eventually, and they died fairly young.

There were times when brother Bill and I didn't mind helping Doughertys with their work, because sometimes they had a beautiful girl named Maryann Fitzpatrick visiting, and we liked being in her presence. One time when she was there, we worked for several days, after which Bill Dougherty and Tucker took about 8 of us in the back of Tucker's pickup truck to an amusement park on Oneida lake. When we got there, Bill gave Maryann ten dollars for us to spend. We were all happy, because nobody had any money, and ten dollars would take us a long ways. We walked around a bit, and when it came time to spend some money, we turned to Maryann, and guess what? She lost the money! Now we were a rough lot, and if anyone else had lost the money they would have paid a high price. But because it was Maryann, we forgave her, and just wandered around until the men came back from their beer drinking and picked us up. We told them what a great time we had, and never admitted losing the money.

The Dougherty family were not just neighbors. They were considered relatives as well, since my Grandpa Danehy's first wife was a Dougherty, and my Aunt Mary, described later, was a blood relative of the Doughertys. As a little kid, I remember going up there, and being with "Uncle" Jim and "Aunt" Nell, Bill Dougherty's parents, and "Uncle " Johnny, Bill's uncle. One time I was in the side yard up there, when one of their roosters attacked me. I must have been about 4 or 5 years old and started yelling and crying. Uncle Johnny came charging out of the wood shed with an ax, grabbed the rooster, and proceeded to behead the miserable beast on a nearby stump. I still remember thinking that justice was done.

One last Dougherty story: Our family was invited to a picnic at their house one Sunday afternoon in the summer. My mother struggled to get us ready and half-way clean, and we loaded into the car in high spirits. When we arrived, Ma opened the car door just in time to hear somebody say, "who invited the Danehys?" as we all tumbled out of the car and started raising hell. I guess we had a reputation, especially Bill and me, but we have laughed about that many times since, and my friends still say, "WHO INVITED THE DANEHYS" when Sue and I arrive at a party.

You read a lot today about spouse abuse, and its effects on women. Well, my experience was a little different. My memories are of several neighbors, like Stanley Pickard and Claude Rouse, not to mention Dad on an occasion or two, who would come home loaded to the gills, at which time their wives would give them a good beating (a verbal lashing in Ma's case), but Claude suffered some occasional damage. So I thought spouse abuse was when the wife beat up the husband! Wrong again.

26

Dad's Relatives

Probably the most important relatives in our very early lives were Grandpa Will and Grandma Liz Danehy. We shared the farmhouse with them. They had the front downstairs and we had the back downstairs and the whole upstairs. It was a big, drafty old house, but lots of room for everyone. We even had two toilets! More later on this important topic. The house was a two story "colonial" with additional rooms in the back and a big porch off one side.

Grandpa Danehy was crippled and ill besides, for most of the time I knew him. He was good to us kids, though, and we enjoyed being with him. Grandpa was married twice, first to a Dougherty,

Grandpa Will and Grandma Liz (Casey) Danehy, circa 1945.

who died in childbirth, then to my Grandmother, who was a Casey. I think Grandpa was a dyed-in-the-wool Republican, because when F. D. Roosevelt died in 1945, Bill Dougherty came rushing into the driveway, saying, "Uncle Will, Roosevelt just died." Grandpa, who was sitting in the yard resting, said, "it's a God-damned good thing." I don't know why he felt so strongly, but he sure did.

Grandma Danehy was also nice to us, but there was always a little tension between Grandma and Ma. A lot of the reasons I don't know about, but it could not have been easy for two families to share a house, especially when one of the families had five runny nosed, noisy little kids making a mess of things.

Dad (center) at Kansas City Aeronautical Institute.

I guess this is the place to tell you about the real trouble our family got into when Grandpa died. My father came home to the farm in the early 1930's when Grandpa got sick. (Dad was at the Kansas City Aeronautical Institute at the time after having left Syracuse University due to wine, women, and song.) The farm was in great shape at the time, having come through the Depression unscathed. Dad was not real happy about this change in plans, and as hard as he worked at farming, I don't think he ever totally had his heart in it, and farming is a poor work choice if you are not sold on it as a way of life.

Anyway, things went well until Grandpa died in 1948. Then it was discovered that he did not have a will, which under New York State law meant that Grandma inherited 1/3 of the estate, and the children split the other 2/3. I think Dad and Mom wound up with 1/6 of the estate. I still remember the auction, necessary to pay the other relatives. Dad wound up with just enough money to buy the property. No cows, no machinery, no nothing. I don't pretend to know all the details of what happened, but I have always admired my parents for maintaining very close relationships with all those involved in the breakup of the farm. I'm not sure I could have maintained such a forgiving attitude.

Well, we were poor after that for a while. Dad had to seek work off the farm, and work was hard to find. He worked on construction, and at a rendering plant in Syracuse. If you don't know what a rendering plant is, consider yourself fortunate. You could smell it and anyone who worked there from miles away. Dad didn't always come home right after work during those times, and I remember Mom being pretty unhappy, and a few big arguments. After a few years, Dad finally bought some cows, but they weren't very good milkers, and we were still pretty poor for a while. I remember going to town with Dad one day and asking him for a quarter. He said if he had a quarter, he would have given it to me. He was broke. Eventually, he built the herd quality up, Ma went back to teaching in Chittenango, and things started looking up.

The Pickards- The only other nearby relatives were Uncle Charlie and Aunt Sue Pickard, described earlier, and their three kids, Marianne, Chuckie, and Rosie. Our families spent a lot of time together, working and for meals, drinks, and relaxation. They always had more "stuff" than we did, including a freezer full of ice cream at a time when most of our refrigerators had no or very small freezer compartments. I used to mow their lawn with a hand mower. I also mowed our own, but theirs was more memorable because I got paid. They also paid me to babysit. I babysat for three families. As mentioned earlier, I had specific babysitting standards, which included lots of snacks, and one daughter old enough to change diapers and get me snacks. The Pickards met the qualifications, as Marianne was about 10 years old, and their freezer was full of ice cream.

One interesting character at the Pickard house was Bog. Bog's real name was H. L. Pickard, and he was Uncle Charlie Pickard's father. He lived in the cellar, along with the potatoes, barrels of hard cider, and other storage items. I never saw him because he never came upstairs, and I sure as heck didn't go down there. I remember him coughing and growling, and that's all. They carried food down to him at meal times. They told a story about Bog, on an occasion when he came out of the cellar.

The Pickards had a mean old bull, and decided to get rid of it at the auction barn in Vernon. They tried to load the bull in a truck, but he got away and was chasing everyone around the farm yard. They thought they were going to have to shoot the bull. Bog heard all the commotion, and came up to see what was happening. He took one look, then said, "Why, you damn fools, go get a cow." They brought out a cow on a lead rope, the bull immediately turned his attention to amorous pursuits, and easily followed as they walked the cow back to the barn. The bull was then more securely tied, and eventually took the ride to Vernon.

Another hanger-on at Pickard's was an old man named Pat Pickard. I would guess that he might have been Bog's brother, but I'm not sure. Pat had no place to stay, so they let him stay at their farm. He didn't like living with other people, so he took an old hay wagon and built a one room shanty on it, using old lumber, and covered with tar paper. He had a stove in there, but no insulation so far as I knew. It must have been pretty drafty in there in the winter, with temperatures near zero and lots of wind.

Uncle Charlie and Aunt Cora Argersinger- Cora was my Grandpa Will's sister. Cora and Charlie lived about four miles away, north toward Canastota. They had three children, two of whom had problems. Rita had Down syndrome. She was a cheerful person who loved to play cards, especially pitch. Tommy was a sad person. My recollection is that Aunt Cora fell from a buggy while pregnant and Tommy was born brain-injured. He was a tall man, who sat in a rocking chair making a ("huh") noise and slapping his hand or his knee with a leather strap. The third daughter, Maryellen, was very normal and very bright. She now lives in Atlanta.

Anyway, back to Uncle Charlie. Bill and I would work hard to finish our field work (haying and threshing), thinking that we would then be able to go to town, or go fishing, or do something fun, right? Wrong. Dad would announce that we were going to help Uncle Charlie with his threshing. Now we didn't like this news for a variety of reasons. Dad was always volunteering for these projects, but we especially disliked going to Argersingers because he was mean, he had lots of money and could have hired his work done, he was tighter than bark to a tree, his equipment was antique, he knew we liked Pepsi, but we were lucky if we got water, and he didn't pay us a red cent. One day Dad took a big crew of us down there; Charlie gave Dad ten dollars to buy food for lunch, and when Dad got back with the food, Charlie asked him where was the change? That did it. The next year we refused to go there to work. The old skinflint must have had to dust off a few bills to pay somebody after that.

Dennis Danehy- When we got done with haying, it was often time to go do Dennis Danehy's work. This was another job we hated, but for different reasons. Dennis was really poor and needed the help. Dennis was a cousin of Dad's. Dennis must have been the son of Pete or John, mentioned elsewhere in this document. Dennis was married (I think) to Mabel, and they had a son Wallace. This was a pitiful group. They lived in a shack on a small farm near Peterboro, about six miles away. The place was dirty and rundown. I don't know if they had electricity or running water, because we (Bill and I) refused to go in the place. Anyway, we went there to do their haying. After working for a few hours, much to our horror, out came Dennis and Mabel with tea for us in a gallon jug. We told them we had just finished drinking water and couldn't hold another drop.

One Thanksgiving, Dad stopped to see them. They were a mess. He came home, took the turkey Ma was baking for us, and took it over to them. I don't remember what we did, but we didn't go hungry, that's for sure.

A few years later, Dennis died. Apparently, Dennis never took his boots off in the winter. Unfortunately, they were rough felt-lined boots, his legs became infected, and he died of gangrene. I don't know what happened to Mabel, but Wallace, who was retarded in some way, wound up in a nursing home. A sad story all around.

Aunt Mary Danehy was one of the more interesting relatives. My Dad's sister, half-sister really, was a school teacher in Utica. She was very nice to us kids, but eccentric, opinionated, and toward the end, out of control. She never married, drove Buick cars, and went to church whenever possible. She used to babysit us sometimes, for reasons I can't understand, as we raised Hell when she was there. Our house was built such that you could go from the kitchen to the living room to the porch and then through a window (if it was open) back to the kitchen. One day a bunch of us were running around this circle.

Aunt Mary in her prime, seated left, with Mary Dougherty; Dad and Aunt Alyce standing.

Aunt Mary told us to stop. We paid no attention so she started to chase us. We jumped through the window and closed it. She didn't see it and hit the window, breaking it. I don't remember any blood, so I guess she was not hurt, but I do remember getting the usual butt-kicking when Dad got home.

Aunt Mary was religious. She filled her car radiator with holy water, and carried holy water with her in the car. Once her car caught on fire and she put it out with holy water, so being religious paid off. Another time, Aunt Mary and one Mary Dougherty were in Cazenovia shopping. She never locked her car (nobody did back then) and unknown to them, a drunk climbed into the back seat and went to sleep. Along toward dark, they got back to the car, climbed in, and drove the 8 miles out to the Dougherty farm. At that point Mary Dougherty said, "my God, there's a man in the car," started screaming, and ran in the house. Aunt Mary, on the other hand, grabbed a stick and started beating on the man and telling him to start running while he still could! The last she saw of him, he was running full speed out across the fields in the dark. Don't you wonder what that guy was thinking, and whether he ever got back to town?

When Aunt Mary got old, things went downhill. The doctor told her to stop drinking whiskey, so she switched to bourbon. She would come in, sit down, and say, "get me a drink." Please and thank you had left her vocabulary. She must have been about eighty by then but still going strong. She went to the Holy Land on a tour, and got back in Syracuse at about midnight. I had the bad luck of going to get her. She insisted on going out to eat. I

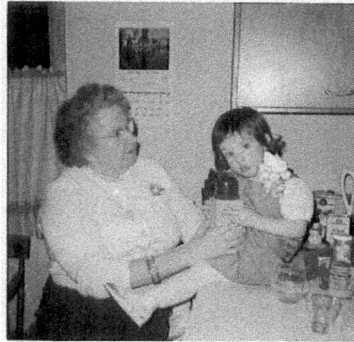

Aunt Mary and Cathy Danehy, circa 1967.

told her all the restaurants were closed. "No, they're not," she said. So we drove all over Central New York trying to humor her, until I got really exasperated and dropped her off at the Martins, where she was staying. A difficult woman, indeed!

My sister Patsy, Paul Martin, and Marianne Pickard Dygert

became her caregivers when she got quite bad. She lived at the Catholic Women's Club in Utica. She got to the point where she was pretty well broke, partially because she was contributing large amounts to various Republican national figures, such as Jesse Helms. She also got invited to Ronald Reagan's Inauguration, whatever that cost her. Once Patsy Hagan and I went down to get her for a Thanksgiving dinner at Mom and Dad's. I sat in the car while Patsy went in to get her. It must have been close to an hour, even though we told her to be ready when we got there. When she finally came out, she said if she had known I was waiting, she would have sent down the paper for me to finish. I said I would have had time to read *Gone with the Wind*.

The Tupperware Christmas with Aunt Mary.

As she got more eccentric, she did some funny things, such as giving everyone the same slightly inappropriate or useless thing for Christmas. Naturally we all made fun of her for that. For instance one year she gave everyone, man, woman, and child, a Tupperware container. We all put them on our heads and wore them as hats for the evening. Eventually, Aunt Mary had to go to a nursing home. I went down to help finish cleaning out her apartment. Although she was always a little cluttered in her housekeeping, near the end it was really bad. We called the Salvation Army to come and take her furniture. The truck pulled up in front and these two beat-up-looking guys came in to look things over. They took a lamp and a couple pillows out to the truck. The next thing we heard was the engine starting. I looked out just in time to see the truck disappear around the corner. So much for Aunt Mary's furniture.

Before the politicians and the nursing home got all her money,

PJ and Patsy managed to put a little bit aside for a slush fund. Since her death, we have used most of it for some very nice "Aunt Mary parties," which she would have approved of, I am sure.

We had a long and involved relationship with Aunt Alyce and Uncle Charlie Martin and their five boys. Bill and I went separately to Watertown each summer to spend a week with them. It was our big outing for the year. Watertown had five movie theaters, and we tried to get to all of them. It was the big city to us, and we enjoyed the experience. I especially remember standing on the bridge over the roaring Black River, and being afraid of falling into that swirling, dark water.

Anyway, when they came to the farm, all hell broke loose, and we had a great time. Charlie was quite a bit older than us, and he spent most of his time chasing the Ingram girls, our neighbors. Jack was next, and a true hell raiser from start to finish. One year when they pulled in, he got so excited he punched me in the stomach and laid me out on the lawn for a few minutes. It still hurts. Jack drank beer when he was 16, and Dad and the neighbor gang didn't discourage him. He was big for 16, and once they were all in Fazio's in Canastota, and Jack ordered a beer. When asked if he was 18, he said yes and got his beer. A little later, they were talking about getting drafted into the army, and Jack told the bartender he didn't have

PJ, Sue, Mary Lee and Mike after a successful fishing trip.

to worry about that for two more years. Oops! No more beer for Jack. Jack went to The U.S. Military Academy. I am still sad when I write that Jack was killed in action in Vietnam during the Tet offensive in 1967.

Aunt Alyce and Uncle Charlie had a long and stormy relationship which never would have lasted in today's society. Most of their troubles were due to not enough money and too much alcohol, a theme which seems to run through a lot of this narrative. Anyway, they were always good to us as kids, and did Sue and me a lot of favors as adults. More elsewhere on that.

Donnie was the third Martin. He was different from the others, not as rough and tumble, and not interested in the farm or all the trouble we could get into on the farm.

Now Jim was another story. He was a lot like Jack, about my age, and we got in plenty of trouble when Jim was around. He was a good athlete, and had a good pitching arm. One time Dad hired a crew to build a new sixty-foot silo. One of the men on the crew who was up on top of the silo hollered down to me to ask my father for a left-handed cement saw. I ran up to where my father and some neighbors were chewing the fat and asked for a left-handed cement saw. They all had a great laugh at my expense, at which point I realized there was no such thing. I sulked away, very angry and very embarrassed. Jim Martin was there, and when I told him what happened, we proceeded out to the barnyard and swore at the crew, who had a good laugh at my expense. Jim picked up a good-sized rock and pegged it up to the top of the silo, hitting one of the workers in the head and nearly knocking him off the silo. They didn't think it was so funny after that. Well, we were severely punished, but it was worth it.

Paul (PJ) was probably the cousin I spent most time with, then and even now. PJ had a long career as a New York State Bank Examiner, and now lives a well organized life in Florida. However, as a boy, PJ could hang in there with the best of them at the bar. We had many good times, at parties on the farm, and later on when we would go fishing in the North Country. We would constantly argue about whether to troll or still fish, whether to fish in deep water or shallow, what bait to use, what speed to troll, was it going to rain, etc. The only time I can remember us agreeing was when PJ drove a fishhook all the way through his thumb. We both agreed we should quit fishing for the day and get PJ to the emergency room!

Uncle Charlie was a serious smoker, and over time he developed a consuming cough, which we all ignored, even though it was a racking cough and went on and on. One Christmas vacation when I was home from college, the Martins were visiting, and Suzanne, a junior at Syracuse University was part of the family by then. Sue invited her old roommate, Muriel, and Muriel's boyfriend Fred to stop in at our house for a *short* visit. They were nice people, but very proper and definitely nondrinkers and nonsmokers. There were a bunch of us sitting around in the kitchen, drinking beer and some hard cider Dad had brewed up, and Uncle Charlie was chain smoking his cigarettes. The afternoon wore on, and Ma, being Ma, invited Muriel and Fred to stay for supper. Sue had been in the family long enough to know that this was probably a bad idea and tried to wave her off, but they quickly accepted the invitation. After more beer, cider, and conversation, dinner was served. Muriel and Fred were sitting directly across from Uncle Charlie. It was a big table in the big kitchen, and I would say there were about 15 of us eating. Anyway, Uncle Charlie got into a real coughing fit. He coughed and hacked, and leaned over in his chair, and his head was sinking lower and lower as he coughed. Meanwhile, the rest of us (except Muriel and Fred) just kept on eating and talking as if nothing unusual was happening. They just sat there wide-eyed and incredulous. Eventually, Uncle Charlie stopped coughing and went on with his meal. Muriel and Fred left as soon as they could get out from behind the table. That was in 1959, and Sue hasn't seen or heard from them since!

*Getting on toward dinner at the farm;
Uncle Charlie is in the white shirt and
glasses.*

Uncle Charlie and Aunt Alyce were involved with the Mike and Sue Danehy family on many occasions. I was very unhappy working for Firestone in Akron, Ohio, in 1963, when we came home to a family reunion. When I told Aunt Alyce I was looking for a job, she told me there was a teaching opening for an Engineer at Canton ATC, where she taught. I called the same day, and within a week had a new job and a new outlook on life, thanks to them. They even rented our first house in Canton for us, sight unseen by us. Come to think of it, they did the same thing for us years later when I took a sabbatical in Florida, and they rented a house for us near where they lived.

We eventually moved to a house next door to them in Canton, and we had many good times together, and a few very sad times, notably when Jack was killed in Vietnam, and we were next door and shared their great grief over this loss. We shared a driveway with them, and Pa Martin used to be a little upset when the driveway was littered with tricycles, carts, and other toys, but he never said much. Our cats used to climb on his freshly washed car with muddy paws, and that didn't go over too big either, but he was pretty calm about that compared to the time he left his window open and the cat curled up for a rest on his good hat. We made up for that by having them over for dinner a lot.

Sometimes we would have him over when Aunt Alyce was gone away. He would come even if he didn't like what we were having. He would always say, "Any old port in a storm." Usually, though, when he was finished, he would say, "That was a noble repast." They were always very kind to us and we valued their friendship greatly.

Dad had many other relatives who came around to the farm fairly often. One was Uncle Tim, a crotchety old man, crippled to the point where I never saw him walk. He was my Grandpa Will's brother. He was the only one of Grandfather's brothers that I remember. John

Grandpa's brothers: John, Will, Pete and Tim.

and Pete were out there somewhere, but they were apparently not close like the Casey relatives and all the Ryan gang on my mother's side of the family. Uncle Tim was not a favorite with anyone except Aunt Mary. My main memory of him was when he ran over my bicycle with his car. Now you know why he was not a favorite of mine.

Lots of adult Casey relatives came to visit. Most of them lived in or near Syracuse. Some of them were fun and great storytellers. Others liked to give orders and tell Bill and me what to do. We, of course, paid no attention to them.

The House and Barn

The old Danehy farm house needs more description. It is in sad repair now, and will soon fall down, but it was a great house to grow up in. It is partially described elsewhere, but more detail is needed. For instance, although there were five large bedrooms, there were absolutely no closets in the house, except for one or two small cubbyholes in hallways, used mostly to store towels and bedding. I finally nailed a broomstick across the corner of my room upstairs, where I hung a few clothes. Ma and Dad had a wardrobe to store their clothes in, but we kids made do with old dressers. I used to climb into Ma's wardrobe and curl up on the clothes stored in there. I liked the smell in there. There was no toilet upstairs, so Ma kept a "chamber pot" in the back hall which we used at night. I don't know who emptied it, but it wasn't me!

The foundation of the house was made of large limestone rocks, piled tightly together but with no mortar to hold them together. The wind would blow through into the cellar in winter, so we piled horse manure and straw up against the house each fall, and removed it in spring. After we got a hay baler, we piled bales against the foundation instead.

The woodshed was connected to the kitchen, and we almost always entered the house through the woodshed. It was a big room, used to store everything under the sun, including wood for the stoves, outgoing trash, dirty barn clothes awaiting washing, shoes, lots of boots, the chunk stoves in summer, and more. One time when we were about four or five years old, Ma and Dad left Bill and me with Grandpa Will, which was a mistake. He was crippled, and a little deaf, and just sat in his chair in the front living room. We decided to do Ma and Dad a favor, and clean the woodshed, which really needed it. We then proceeded to take everything we could lift, and throw it in a big pile in the kitchen. Soon the woodshed was spic and span, and the parents arrived home. At first they were proud of us, but then they opened the door into the kitchen and saw the awful mess piled there. I don't remember what our punishment was, but we never had Grandpa for a sitter again. That kitchen door reminds me of yet another fight with Bill. We got in a fight, and he ran in through the woodshed to the kitchen, and locked the door so I couldn't get in. I grabbed an ax and started wailing away at the door until I got tired. It was a very thick heavy door, and I didn't do much damage, but you can still see the deep gouges in the wood.

Bill and I were always trying to improve things on the farm. One day when we were three or four years old, Ma got us all dressed up in our best clothes and told us to wait in the yard while she got dressed, and don't get dirty. We went down to the horse barn and spied some milk cans which looked like they could use a coat of paint. Luckily, we found a large can of green paint and some brushes nearby, and proceeded to paint the cans. I was never a neat painter, and this was no exception. By the time Ma found us, we were covered with paint and the milk cans were ruined, along with our clothes. Ma was mad about the clothes, Dad was mad about the milk cans, and we were mad because they didn't appreciate our work. I assume we got a few lashes for that one.

The kitchen was big and friendly, and a lot of good meals were served there, but it was also where the worst activity of the week took place, namely wash day. There were huge piles of clothes to wash, for five kids, two adults, and assorted hired men and hangers-on. Almost all the work fell on Ma, and I remember well the drudgery she went through on wash day. She did have a wringer washer, which thrashed the clothes around, after which she ran them through the wringer to squeeze out the water. Then it was time to hang them on the clothes line, which was okay in summer, but in winter you wound up with frozen overalls which stood up by themselves when you brought them in the house. She must have been exhausted after that, but then it was time to stoke up the cook stove and get supper ready for the men!

That back hall really was a dark, creepy place. No wonder Patsy hated it. It had other ghosts besides Bill and me. The floors creaked, and there was old furniture, beds, boxes, broken windows, and other stuff piled around up there. At one time, a hired man named Bill O'Brien slept up there. One morning he didn't get up, so Bill went up to check on him, but he was dead! He "liked the drink," and drank wood alcohol, which was used as antifreeze during WWII. It would give you a good buzz, but was poison. His ghost kind of hung in the air up there from then on.

Another death on the farm occurred shortly before I was born. Some of Dad's Casey relatives came to visit, and while they were there, the husband of one of the Casey women couldn't be found, so they sent Dad looking for him. Dad looked in the horse barn, and there he was, hanging from a rafter. The story I heard was that he was married to one of the Casey women, but was in love with her sister. The situation apparently became too painful for him to endure.

The barn was a great place for young lads growing up. It was actually several barns all connected together in a line, with one section off at right angles. The barn had pine boards for siding, and most of it had a metal roof. I remember painting that entire barn one summer. We all pitched in when we could, and it still took all summer. It probably hadn't been painted in 30 years, and it sucked up paint. I think Dad hired some rednecks to paint it, but they were soon fired due to poor workmanship, so Dad put his own rednecks (us) to work to finish the job. He bought paint in 5 gallon cans, and plenty of them. What a job. As a reward, he had us paint the house, which was in even worse shape, the next summer. I grew up with a great dislike of painting.

The hay barn had beams and columns all over the place, and these were great for climbing. Usually there was hay in the barn to catch you if you fell, or more often, were pushed, but it was still dangerous up there. We usually had a basketball hoop set up in the barn, and we played until we got in a fight, which was often.

The cow barn was in the basement of the barn. The cows were lined up in two rows, with a gutter behind them and a feeding manger in front. I didn't like cows, and didn't like to milk, so Bill usually milked while I climbed the silo, threw down ensilage, fed the cows corn, hay, and other nutrients, and fed the calves. The cow barn holds many memories, mostly not so good. In summer, the flies were so thick you had to hold your breath not to inhale them. In winter, the space where the cows stayed was actually fairly warm due to body heat, but the side rooms were nasty cold.

Times have changed on farms in many ways, including cleanliness. We dumped milk from the milking machine into pails, then carried the pails to the milk house where we dumped the pail into milk cans. It was not unusual for a cow to kick a leg coated with manure near a pail, or even step in a pail if we were milking by hand. Never mind, that milk got poured right in with the rest. All farms now have a toilet in the barn, but back then many people didn't even have one in the house. Therefore, we always had a Sears Roebuck catalog in the barn, and Dad and other people I won't name routinely used the gutter for a toilet, with the catalog serving both as reading material and for cleanup.

We were not friends with our cows. If they were nice to us, we were nice to them. However, if they tried to kick us when we milked them, we would tie a rope to their tail, throw the rope over a beam in the ceiling, and pull down. This lifted the tail up, was painful, and stopped the cow from kicking. It was mean, but it was survival of the fittest.

Dad tried at times to raise cash crops, mostly peas, but one year he raised cabbage, and a fine crop it was. The problem was that everyone had a great crop of cabbage that year. They harvested a great big truck load of cabbage, and drove off to the canning factory in triumph. Soon they were back, swearing and cussing, because their entire load was only worth a few dollars. Dad refused to sell it, and wound up dumping the whole load down over the rocks behind the barn. I never had any trouble understanding the laws of supply and demand after that. Ever after that, until the day he died, Dad would go wild when Ma bought cabbage at the store, and paid more for one head than he was offered for that whole load!

Dad was not always politically correct. Almost every morning, he would say, "Here come the Jews!" The calf buyers were Jews. They stopped by almost every day, and when a bull calf was born, they bought it for beef. Dad and the calf buyers would yell at each other, wave their arms, and practically fight over the price to pay for the calves. He really liked those men, but until the end it was, "Here come the Jews."

The old farm, 2006.

Well, it's 2014 now, and times change rapidly at the old farm. I heard recently that the barn finally fell down, and the house will follow soon. A big farmer uses all the land, but has no use for the old buildings. Here is a picture we took in 2006. Compare it with other pictures in this narrative to see how times do change. Maybe my own pictures show the same pattern: what do you think?

Harvest time was always big on the farm. I know I have already described some parts of it elsewhere, but each season had its own interests and problems. "Threshing" was a big project in late summer. All the neighbors would get together and share equipment for this job. The ripe oats and wheat were cut and formed into bundles by a horse drawn grain binder. The bundles were stacked up to dry in the field. I wish we had some pictures of these fields, as they were very pretty to see. At this point we prayed for dry weather, as a rain meant going back out and knocking down all the bundles, and start the drying process over again. The dried bundles were forked onto wagons, and taken to the barn, where they were run through the threshing machine, a big, noisy, very dusty machine which separated the grain from the straw, and blew the straw up into the barn. We always feared rocks in the straw, as it was very dusty, and one spark when a rock hit the fan blade could start a bad fire. I remember at least one bad fire in a barn on a nearby farm, which burned the barn and killed some cattle. As time passed, tractors replaced the horses, and soon combines replaced the threshing machines. You still see one sitting out in some field, looking forlorn and useless. One last comment on this. Uncle Charlie Argersinger, mentioned fondly in an earlier chapter, had a *wooden* threshing machine which must have been one of the first ever built!

The other major harvest occurred in the fall, when corn was ready for harvest. The corn was cut and tied in bundles by a horse drawn corn binder, and the bundles were immediately loaded on wagons and taken to the barn where they were run through an ensilage cutter which chopped up the corn and blew it into the silo. Some of this process was much like harvesting oats, except the bundles were much heavier, and everything was wet instead of dusty. Again, after a few years the horses disappeared, and the corn binder was replaced by a forage chopper which cut and chopped the corn in the field.

Perryville School

Perryville School, circa 1946.

All five of us went to school in Perryville. It's a miracle any of us made it through high school. Mary Ellen won all the prizes in her class every year. We all thought she was really smart until her class went to the "big" school in Cazenovia, at which point everyone in her class except her was placed in the remedial class.

I entertained myself as best I could in Perryville. One tactic was not to go to school. I used to get really bad headaches in the morning. My mother, always the loving soul, would prop me up on a pillow with a warm damp cloth on my forehead. These headaches would disappear as soon as the bus left, and so became known as school bus headaches. One year I missed 45 days with school bus headaches.

I got my first and only knockout at Perryville. I must admit that I used to fight a lot, as you will see. Small disagreements quickly led to physical confrontations, usually wrestling around on the ground until we got tired, but once in a while, a punch or two. Anyway, Alan Snyder, a friend of brother Bill and mine, said something I didn't like, so I punched him in the jaw, his eyes rolled up, and down he went. We were all shocked! He woke right up, and we went on with whatever game we were playing. I suppose if that happened today, I would be suspended and sent to reform school. Well, more fights later.

Mike, circa 1946.

We did some really bad things at Perryville. Once, we brought bullets to school. Then we got two rocks and pounded on the bullets, trying to get them to go off. Nothing happened. Another time we brought matches to school. We found a few holes drilled in the side of the wooden building, so proceeded to light the matches and drop them through the holes. Why the place didn't catch on fire is beyond me. What were we thinking?

One sad thing I remember at Perryville was the poor way that mentally handicapped kids were treated. As far as I can recall, they just did not go to school. I remember one boy in particular, named Bummy Kimple, who used to stand around out in the schoolyard looking in the window, with his sack of bottle caps over his shoulder. He spent his time wandering around town picking up bottle caps, just for something to do.

Inside the school, there were four grades, all in one room, four in each grade, and one teacher who was usually about half there. At least one had a complete breakdown while I was there, and as we used to say, "went to Marcy." Marcy was the state mental hospital. Each grade of four kids would come up to the front of the room and sit on a bench to recite with the teacher. One day I pushed back with my feet, the bench tipped backwards, and all four of us fell on the floor. As punishment for that one, the teacher made me sit in the wastebasket. My knees were up next to my ears! That was the last time I tipped over the bench.

Riding the Bus

After finishing fourth grade I rode the bus 10 miles to Cazenovia to the "big" school. My friends "Pick" and Dave and Bill and I had many adventures on the bus. The bus route took us through Fenner township, a high, windy country of fields and forests, with scattered farms, lots of cows, and lots of snow in the winter. It was sometimes in doubt whether we would get home in the evening. I can remember hanging out the door watching for the edge of the road, telling the bus driver, who could see nothing, if he was too close to the ditch. On another occasion, when we were still quite young, maybe nine or so, the bus got completely stuck about a mile from our house, and we walked home through a howling blizzard.

Fenner in winter: a stalled train.

We were an unruly group on our bus. One kid, Walt Christenson, was especially bad. He hated school, swore like a trooper, and fought going to school every day. One day his mother wrestled him onto the bus, the bus driver closed the door and away we went. It was the day of a food drive, and Walt had a can of soup in a bag in the overhead rack. He kept yelling and swearing, so the driver stopped the bus and came back to where Walt was sitting. Walt, who was about ten at the time, reached up, grabbed the soup, and hit the bus driver in the head! I honestly don't recall what happened next, but I know it wasn't good.

One more story about Walt. Walt had several sisters who were very nice and easy to look at besides. In fact, I recently saw one of them at my 50th high school reunion, and she is still nice, and still pretty.

Anyway, we used to go see the girls sometimes when we were in high school. We were there one day when Walt and his sidekick "Squeak" Roberts were repairing the barn cleaner. Now you non-farmers need to know that this machine runs along in the gutter behind the cows and carries the manure out to a manure spreader. Repairs to this machine require a strong nose and a high tolerance for poop!

Well, lunchtime came along and we were invited to stay. Never ones to turn down a free meal, we were enjoying lunch, when in came Walt and Squeak, straight from the barn, and helped themselves to a sandwich or two, without any stop to wash up. Yes sir, Walt was a tough customer.

Back to the bus. The driver Walt hit with the soup was named Snyder. He only had one hand; well, he had a second hand, but no fingers. We gave him and some other drivers quite a hard time. Once someone wadded up their leftover lunch in waxed paper and threw it up to the front, hitting the windshield. Once Snyder kicked Pick and Dave off the bus before we even left Cazenovia, and left them ten miles from home. When we got to Pick's house, next door to our house, there were Pick and Dave in the front yard, laughing and waving. They hitch-hiked and beat us home! Snyder couldn't win.

Snyder's career as a bus driver ended when he brought a case of beer on the bus with him. Soon after, he was gone.

Fights

Fights were a big part of growing up for me. Lots of fights were all in fun, with teams. Others were planned, but most were just my common reaction to conflict. I must say that I do not remember ever getting really hurt fighting, nor do I remember hurting anyone. It must have been mostly rolling around on the ground until everyone was tired! Things which get kids suspended from school today were not much of a problem then. I remember the teacher in charge of the playground telling us if we were going to fight, to go up behind the playground storage shed where he couldn't see us.

Me and Bill and Pick and Dave, and sometimes others, often had team "fights." We would choose sides and go at it. Once we had a B-B gun fight in the hay barn. We got behind bales of hay and blasted away at each other. Dave got in a pattern of jumping up, shooting, and ducking down. I timed him and shot just as he jumped up, hitting him in the soft skin near his eye. Needless to say, no more B-B gun fights and another tongue lashing for Mike and Bill.

Other times we would chase each other through the barns throwing apples or corncobs, or once in awhile, horse poop, which, as you know is round and fairly firm. We were not very careful and sometimes got hurt. The hay barns were above the cow barns, and holes were cut in the floor to drop the hay down. These holes were covered unless somebody forgot, or put the cover on crooked. Once in our barn, a cover was on crooked and I ran on to the edge of it. It pivoted and whacked me in the head as I fell through the hole and landed on the floor below. No broken bones, but a big goose egg on my forehead. Once during a corncob fight in Pick's barn, I ran full speed through an open hole and fell to the concrete floor below. That time I did break my arm.

When I went to the big school in Cazenovia I was involved in a lot of fights. The town kids would call me "farmer," resulting in immediate fisticuffs and wrestling (mostly wrestling). Other times, when choosing sides for softball, one false move would set off a fight. We had a teacher named Max Buckley who had playground duty. His rule on fighting was that if we wanted to fight, we had to go up behind a shed where he couldn't see us. Good rule, huh? I remember one long series of fights, with me and Pick against the world. Pick had a wool hat (his only hat) knit with black and white stripes. Every noon, we would go outside, someone would call Pick "skunk head," and the fight would be on. I can remember looking forward to noon hour with great enthusiasm. The only time I remember a problem fighting at school was when I got in a fight with another kid from Perryville named Jimmy Van Alstyne. He was a little kid, but two bad things happened to me. He had a big, mean guy for a friend, and Jimmy bit me on the arm and wouldn't let go. The big kid said if I hit Jimmy, he would beat me up, so I gave up. What could I do?

I had a few minor fights in high school, the worst of which was with my brother Bill after school one day as we were getting on the bus. There we were, fighting and swearing, with 500 or so spectators cheering us on!

There are a few other memorable things that happened at school. There was a kid named Donald Morrison who thought he was a truck. The building was three stories tall, and he would start in first gear on the lower floors, and RRREVV his motor and shift gears as he came up to the third floor, where we had math class with Miss Coye, a woman about sixty years old, five feet tall, and weighing about eighty pounds, making her about half Donald's size. Donald came up, making an infernal noise, and rounded the corner by our room...RRRRRR... Miss Coye was waiting. She grabbed him, slammed him against the wall, and gave him a few whacks. After that, Donald drove his truck up other stairwells. My mother's cousin, Miss Durkin, was a social studies teacher at school, but she had no control over the students. Her classroom was next door to Miss Coye. On one occasion, Miss Durkin asked the class a question. Some wise guys in the back poured lighter fluid on their hands, lit it and waved their hands vigorously, which kept the flames from burning them, but certainly got the teacher's attention. She had to call Miss Coye in to restore order. Even the biggest and dumbest kids were afraid of Miss Coye.

Well, the more serious fights were right in the family. I am happy to say that we all get along pretty well now after all the stuff that went on when we were kids. Jim (Dugan) and Mary Ellen weren't in many fights. Mostly, we just did stuff to them. For instance, Dugan had a B-B gun when Bill and I were a little older and our guns were long gone. I convinced him that he should let me take his B-B gun, climb the silo, and shoot the pigeons which were roosting up there. He thought this was a good idea, so up I went. Unfortunately, when I got to the top of the silo, the pigeons flew, startled me and I dropped the B-B gun fifty feet down onto concrete. Sorry, Dugan, it was an accident.

Danehy family, circa 1951.

Fights with Patsy were infrequent but violent. One day Bill and I did the milking in the morning when Ma and Dad were away and Patsy was to make breakfast. We were hungry, and demanded that she hurry up with the meal. Bill said, "I want my bacon!" Patsy said, "OK, here's your bacon," and hit him in the head with a package of bacon she was unwrapping. I think we wound up eating cereal that morning. Another time, we were all late eating breakfast, the bus was coming, and Patsy and I were arguing. I don't remember hitting my sisters any other time, but this day she said something that really made me mad, so I took a swipe at her. I missed her, but hit her cereal bowl full of corn flakes and milk. She was splattered from head to toe, a pitiful sight to see. We were all stunned.

Meanwhile, the bus pulled up out front and started blowing the horn. Bill, Dugan, and Mary Ellen went out, and I soon followed, leaving Ma to help Patsy clean up. She stayed home that day, and I had a very bad day, thinking that I was a lowdown skunk of a brother. She eventually forgave me, because she lets me stay at her house when I go to Cazenovia.

Maybe you wonder why Patsy wasn't more patient with Bill and me. Here is an example. Patsy is afraid of some things, like lightning and very dark places. She still won't stay home alone in a thunder storm, and probably doesn't like the dark. This is why.

Baler problems--hope Dad comes before a fight starts.

On the farm, our bedrooms were upstairs in the front of the house. Because Grandpa and Grandma Danehy lived in the front downstairs, we had to get to our rooms by climbing up a narrow back stairway, walking through a spooky, dark, back room filled with what I would call junk, with no lights until we got to the front of the house. For Bill and me, it was perfect! Lots of places to hide. For Patsy, terror. Bill and I would say we were tired and go up the stairs. Later, Patsy would follow, and we would be in hiding, jump out and scare her out of her wits. Great fun! The conversation would be something like this:

Me and Bill: "Ma, we're tired and are going up to bed."

Patsy: "No, Ma, don't let them go up there. They'll scare me again. Sob. Sob."

Me and Bill: "Ma, we won't scare her. We felt bad last time when she cried and cried."

Ma: "Alright, boys, I believe you and I know you will be nice to your sister. Goodnight."

Patsy: "No, Ma, please, please, sob, sob."

Me and Bill: "Goodnight, Ma. Goodnight, Patsy. Pleasant dreams."

We would then go up the stairs. Later on Patsy would creep up through the dark, where even a flashlight didn't help much, and of course there we were, lurking in the shadows.

Me and Bill: BBOOOO! BBBOOOOOOO!

Patsy: WAAAAAA! WAAAAAA!

Ma: "You boys get down here, now."

Ma: WHACK, WHACK, WHACK

Eventually we quit doing this dirty trick, but maybe not until Grandma and Grandpa were gone and Patsy could get to her room by the front stairs.

The real main events were with Bill. We were just a year apart in age, and though we got along pretty well as little kids, and get along pretty well now, the teenage years through about age 20 were rough. A lot of our fights occurred due to differences of opinion on how to get work done when Dad was not there to supervise, or on how to drive a car in heavy snow, or on where to go to get a beer. Once we were assigned to clean the gutters in the cowbarn. Dad was in the cornfield chopping corn, and all the neighbors were hauling corn to the barn and blowing it into the silo. Bill and I pulled in the manure spreader and pitched in nice juicy manure, one of us working on each side of the spreader. Eventually we started splashing each other, then throwing manure at each other. All the neighbors working on the corn stopped to watch as we sparred with dung forks and shovels, swore, and rolled around in the gutters. The corn harvest came to a screeching halt. Dad sat out in the field wondering what happened. He eventually came in, and that was the end of the fight. It was not unusual for us to fight with forks, shovels, hoses, straps, etc. Don't ask me why we never got hurt, though we were tough, and we must have pulled our punches.

We had a lot of problems with driving in the snow. Bill believed in driving slowly up to a drifted road, and looking things over to see if we could make it. I believed in going fast, thinking we could blast our way through the drifts, which sometimes worked, but when it didn't, left the car high and dry in a drift with all four wheels off the ground. When this happened, it was a matter of extensive shoveling, or more

Mike and Bill, circa 1942.

often, abandoning the car, seeking shelter at a nearby house, and waiting for the snowplow to come through in the morning. I don't know how my mother dealt with this. We never called home, and some of the storms were severe.

One night, we got within a mile from home in a real blizzard. I was driving, and yes, I put us up on a snowbank. We had two snow shovels so got out of the car to start digging out. At least, that is why I thought we got out. I started digging, then "whack," he hit me across the back with his shovel. Then we went at it, right in the middle of the road in a blizzard. A man got stuck a little way behind us, came down the road through the snow, took one look at us and kept right on going. Just down the hill from where we were was Aunt Jessie's house, and the man sought shelter with them. He told them that he had seen a sight to behold up the road. There were two boys swearing and fighting with snow shovels in the middle of the blizzard. "Oh, that's just the Danehy boys," everyone at Aunt Jessie's house agreed.

Once when I was home from college, Bill took me to Cazenovia to catch the bus back to Cornell. I drove his car, and as usual, there was a raging snow storm, and as usual, I drove up on a snowbank part way up a hill. We got out and partially dug out the car. No fight, but plenty of swearing. Bill suggested he get in the car and rock it while I pushed. I agreed, and pushed back on the car, which moved a little. Then he suggested I get behind the car and push ahead, which I did. What I didn't know was that the car was loose and could be easily backed up. When I stepped behind the car, he floored it and tried his best to run over me. I was a little suspicious, so was on guard and jumped out of the way! He lost control and backed the car into the ditch. Anyway, after more shoveling and swearing, we were on our way and I caught the bus.

Bill and I stopped fighting soon after that, when I came home and saw him throw two milk cans full of milk onto a truck at once. I decided at that time that there were other ways to solve our problems.

When Bill left Cornell and went back to the farm to work, he bought a new 1956 Chevy. Soon after, I came home from Cornell for the summer, and got a construction job. I didn't have a car, so the deal was I would take his car to work each day. On the second morning, I went around a corner, my thermos of coffee rolled off the seat, I lunged for it, lost control, and the car went in the ditch. I was going slow, but needless to say, Bill was perturbed, and it cost me my first two weeks pay to fix it.

That car was ill fated. One night Bill and his buddy Snyder were out late. Snyder was a smoker, and on the way home, he threw a cigarette butt out the window of Bill's car. The back window was open, and they didn't notice the butt blow back into the car. Bill came home and went to bed. The next thing I remember is Dad yelling at Bill that his car was on fire. It's the only time I ever remember Bill getting up as soon as he was called. Anyway, it was quite a sight to see Bill out in the driveway in his underwear, shoveling sand from a nearby pile into the back seat of his car.

Alan Snyder and Bill had other adventures. They went out to bars a lot. They got along well because Bill was strong and Snyder had a big mouth. Once they went in a bar down near Sherrill, NY. They had a few beers and Snyder started telling some guy at the bar how tough Bill was, which went over pretty well until the guy pulled a gun, at which time Bill and Snyder left their beer on the bar and headed for the door.

Another time, Snyder was driving. He brought Bill home late at night. Bill told him to drive carefully and went in the house. The windows were open and he could hear the car going up the road, down the hill, around a corner, speed up, then...CRASH!! Bill went to bed, but called Snyder the next morning to see if he was all right. He was, though the car was heavily damaged.

The Weather

I have mentioned how bad the storms could be on the farm, even though the weather was really nice most of the time. In the summer, we sometimes had very bad thunder storms, and in winter, the wind and the snow were bad at times. Wind storms got our attention. We were fearful that the place would blow down, though it never did. Once, Mary Ellen was sitting in the front room during a wind storm, when the wind blew in a large front window, throwing glass across the room. Fortunately, she was sitting behind the big old chunk stove and was not injured.

Another time, the wind blew a large sliding door off its track on the barn, sailed it across the yard, banged it against the house, and finally landed it up on the roof of the house. I sat in the window one day and watched the wind tear down the neighbor's barn, board by board, until the whole thing was flat on the ground and scattered in the fields.

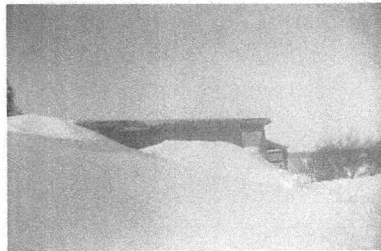

Winter on the farm--the chicken house.

Thunder storms could be very bad on the farm. I remember lightning hitting the water pipes and dancing between the two faucets in the kitchen. Another time, just as I ran from the bus up onto the side porch, a ball of fire hit right on the porch. Don't ask me why there was no blaze. One afternoon there were a series of five or six storms, one after the other, with a lot of rain. A friend of Dad's, Perry Ball, lived near Perryville. After the third or fourth storm, he sent his kid to the store, thinking the storms were over. While the kid was gone, the worst storm of all came along. A dam burst on a stream near the store just as he was crossing the bridge over the stream. He was washed away, swept downstream and over Perryville Falls, a drop of at least 200 feet. It was a day or two before they found his body. The entire village was very upset about that for a long time. We were all a little frightened of the storms. I remember hiding under the kitchen table with the dog, who was also afraid of lightning. Patsy was the champ when it came to being afraid. She was terrified, and still wants nothing to do with thunder storms. I hear that when she hears thunder, if she is alone she gets in the car and heads for the nearest relative. I think that is why she lives in Cazenovia, where relatives abound.

In winter, weather was a constant struggle. Sometimes the cold would freeze the water buckets in the barn, and we would have to water the cows by hand. Sometimes we would take a load of manure out in the fields in a blizzard. The manure spreader threw the manure up in the air behind the spreader as we drove along. In a high wind, the tractor driver sometimes got a nice shower of manure. Once, I remember getting stuck during a blizzard. The spreader sunk down to the axle in soft snow and mud. The only solution was to climb into the spreader, shovel off the manure, then pull away with the empty spreader. If you let it sit there until the storm was over, you risked the weather turning cold, in which case the spreader would have been there until spring.

We loved to go to town, winter storm or not. Bill and I often got stuck on the way home, as I have mentioned, but sometimes one of the others was along. One night when I was 16 or 17, Dugan and I went to town. There was a bad storm raging, but I stayed in town late anyway. I finally picked Dugan up at one of the relatives (we waited for one another at Aunt Peg's or Aunt Jane's houses). We drove home through Fenner when the weather was not too bad, but that was no good this night. We took a longer route through a town called Chittenango when conditions deteriorated, but that road was plugged. Our last chance was to go through Canastota, a much longer trip, probably 25 miles instead of ten via Fenner. I was following another car, visibility near zero, when he went off the road, and

I followed him into the ditch. Finished!

The guy lived a mile or two up the road. I asked if we could stay at his house for the night. He just grunted, but I took that as a yes. When we got to his house, we followed him in, but he paid no attention to us and went upstairs to bed. We could hear his kids coughing and hacking up there. We put our boots near the stove in the kitchen, and Dugan laid down on an old couch. It was cold in there. The wind was blowing through the walls like they weren't even there. I laid down on top of Dugan to keep him warm, but we were both freezing. After a short time, I knew we could not stay there. We got our boots back on. The snow had not melted from the boots. Some heating system. We went back out into the storm. It was better to be out there than in that house. We trudged on down the road. I spotted a light on at a farm house. I knocked on the door, and we were welcomed with open arms. The people, whose name was Yorton, put us in a nice bed with a down comforter, and in the morning served up a big breakfast. By morning, the storm was over, the plows came through and pulled my car out of the ditch, and we were soon home. Once again, I ask how my Mother put up with the stress and worry of us running around the country side in all kinds of terrible weather??

Sliding in the driveway on a sunny day.

Don't get the idea that winter was all bad. When we were younger, we spent a lot of time with our friends, sliding down hill. There sure was lots of snow to keep us going!

Utilities

We had running water from a spring up on the hill in back of the house, and we had not one but two toilets, one in a full bathroom and the other in an old closet. Most of the neighbors had outhouses. These outhouses were usually two holers, and were located in the woodshed just off the kitchen. Tucker and Stanley Pickard both had these systems. You cleaned them by opening a door in the back, but I can tell you that did not happen often. The "stuff" used to pile up in two big cones, although I don't remember them smelling real bad. Either they didn't smell too bad, or we were used to so many bad smells that we paid no attention. Anyway, we were always happy to have real toilets The bathtub had porcelain h o t and cold water handles. I used to duck my head under water and then raise up and watch the water run off the front of my hair. Once I got too close to the front, raised up fast, and broke off one of the faucets in my head. It couldn't have been too serious, because they didn't take me to the doctor, but I still remember the blood, and we lived forever after with a broken faucet.

The side porch in the dead of winter.

As I told you, our water came from a spring up back. The wooden cover on the spring rotted away long ago. Once in awhile in the summer, the water would taste bad and have a real bad smell. We would go up and look in the spring, and there would be a dead woodchuck floating around. We would fish it out, and soon the water would taste better again. Along about 1950 we finally dug a well, which solved our water problems.

Heating the house was a big project. In the kitchen, we had a big stove for cooking and heat. It wouldn't hold a fire over night, so it was cold there every morning until Ma got a fire going. In the two living rooms, we had large chunk stoves, so called because you put large chunks of wood in them. They took up a lot of room, and I remember that we took them out and stored them in the woodshed every spring and dragged them back in every fall.

What a lot of work that was. The stoves had to be carefully tended. If you weren't careful, they would get too hot. They would turn red, and the stove pipe would be glowing all the way up through the hole in the ceiling. We would sit wide eyed as the fire roared and the pipe got hotter and hotter, until somebody shut off the draft, and robbed of oxygen, the fire would calm down. I don't know why we never had a serious fire out of that, though we did sometimes have small chimney fires.

Handwritten note about the new porch, 1942.

Eventually, we got a coal-burning furnace installed in the cellar, with pipes distributing the heat to various rooms. We even had a "stoker" which automatically fed coal to the furnace. That system banged and clanked and made all kinds of noise, but we loved it. No more lugging coal or wood, and no more overheated wood stoves. What we did miss was the enjoyment of sitting around the old stoves when they were working right. It was real warm and cozy when it was cold and stormy outside.

The porch in the photo on the previous page is the "new" enclosed porch built in 1942. I remember the men building the porch, and we enjoyed it a lot, although the old open porch was more fun in good weather. I love the note we ran across recently from Grandpa Will. Handwritten notes make great history!

Cooling the milk was always a problem. Eventually we had an electric milk cooler, but until after WWII we cooled the milk with ice. In the winter, which must have been colder then, the men would go to a nearby lake and cut huge chunks of ice, using a long hand operated saw. These chunks, cubes about two feet on a side, were loaded on a truck using big ice tongs, and brought home to the ice house which was attached to the barn. The ice was stacked up and covered with sawdust as an insulating blanket. The ice lasted easily until the next winter. It was very heavy work, and I only watched, since I was too young to lift the big chunks. I remember the mice loved to live in the sawdust. When you moved a chunk, the mice ran here and there. The cats enjoyed this operation. Free food! The ice kept the milk nice and cold, and we enjoyed drinking milk right out of the milk can covers, with any spillage falling from around our lips and chin back into the can which was shipped off to the milk plant. Thank God for pasteurization.

Telephones were already on the scene when I arrived, and had been for many years, I think. The first telephone I remember was a thing of beauty. It was made of oak, was about the size of a very large shoe box, and was mounted on the wall. It had two bells for a ringer, and a crank on the side for outgoing calls. To call out, you just turned the crank, the operator came on and you told her the number you wanted. Everyone was on party lines. We probably had fifteen people on our party line. All calls to anyone on the party line rang in at every house!! The thing was ringing most of the time. Our number was three long rings and three short rings. You soon got to know all the rings, so if it was anybody interesting, you could pick up and listen to their conversation. The problem was, this caused the quality of reception to deteriorate, and they would know one or more people were listening in (rubbering is what it was called). "GET OFF THE LINE" was probably the most common thing ever heard on those phones.

From three longs and three shorts, we eventually went to a smaller black phone with 923x as a number, but still operator assisted, and then finally to a dial phone and OL52220 as our number for a very long time.

Dog and Other Animal Stories

Some of you may want to skip this part, since dogs and cats were work animals on the farm, and if they didn't work, they didn't last long. On the farm we had about sixty cows, several pigs, three or four horses, sometimes a bull, anywhere from one to twenty cats, one or two dogs, chickens, rats, mice, snakes, woodchucks, etc.

We did love our dogs, and even let them in the house at times. Lassie and Shep were the dogs I remember best. Lassie was a beautiful collie and was around for a long time. Lassie was afraid of thunderstorms, as were all of us, and I remember crawling under the kitchen table with him, and staying there until the storm was well past. It got kind of crowded under there because as I've said, Patsy was afraid of lightning, and Mary Ellen was afraid of

Lassie in the driveway.

everything. Shep was a mongrel shepard mix. Shep had two major problems. Once when he was young, he was lying in the hayfield when Tucker was mowing hay, and Shep had his front leg cut off by the machine. Tucker brought him to the house and we bandaged up the stump. He soon recovered, and got around real well on three legs. No animals except cows ever saw a veterinarian on the farm. Shep then was able to pursue his other passion, which was chasing cars. We tried everything to stop him, but he was hit by cars on several occasions. We would drag him home, and he would recover. I don't remember how he died, but I suspect it was a result of car injuries.

There was also Prince, a nice dog, kind of a beagle mix. We didn't have him long, because somebody fed him chicken bones, and he choked. Life on the farm was rough.

Cats were useful in the barn to keep the mouse and rat population down. They were fed a little milk, but were otherwise on their own. They had a high mortality rate due to disease and being stepped on by cows. When the population got too high, they would die off from disease until only one or two were left. It was fun to find the new litters of kittens in the hay barn, but the mother would move them as soon as she realized we had found her nest. One thing I have never figured out about my parents is why they wouldn't ever let cats in the house. The house was full of mice, and I think a few rats. You could hear them running in the walls and ceilings at night, and it was common to open a drawer in the kitchen or pantry, and have a mouse or two jump out. But no way were there cats in our house. They must have thought the cats were dirty, and would rather live with mice.

Tucker had a few dog problems. Once he had two dogs, one a good cow dog, and the other worthless. He decided to get rid of the bad dog. The usual method was to shoot them. (Sorry, but this is about life on the farm.) Uncle Charlie Pickard was the one who usually did the shooting, so he came up to Tucker's with his rifle. The dog saw him coming and ran under the porch and wouldn't come out. Tucker got a long pole and started poking under the porch, the dog came out, and BANG, Uncle Charlie got him. The only problem was that unbeknown to them, the good dog was under the porch too, and it was he who came out and was killed. Everyone was sad and disgusted by this. I don't know if the bad dog survived or not.

Another time, Tucker and Thumper Rouse, Claude's kid, shot a dog down in the woods behind Tucker's house. Unfortunately, they were seen by someone, who called the cops, and Tucker was arrested. The next day, Thumper was riding on a tractor with Dad, when a trooper drove down into the field to question Thumper, who was about eight years old, about the incident. My Father, for reasons unknown to me, didn't like cops. I think it had something to do with drinking and driving, which Dad did regularly. Anyway, Dad told the cop that unless he had a warrant he could not speak to Thumper, and told him to get off our property, which he did. My memory fails me on the outcome of this incident, but it was one of many in which guns were used to keep the dog population in check. The only excuse for this treatment of animals was that dogs used to pack up if you were not careful, chase cows, and be aggressive around people.

The cows were a necessary nuisance on the farm, since they furnished almost all our income, but they were no fun. They were stupid animals, and while docile most of the time, they would periodically kick you if you weren't careful. I did not like to milk, and usually left that chore to Bill while I fed them ensilage and hay. We had small farm ponds in the neighborhood, and we would be swimming in one end of the pond while the cows were standing in the other end doing what cows do, which is poop and pee. Why didn't we get sick, except for the occasional large boil which required lancing by our friendly family doctor?

I had even less love for the chickens, who had no redeeming value except their eggs. Cleaning the hen house was a smelly, dirty, itchy job which I tried my best to get out of, but with little success. My favorite animals were the pigs, which were docile and only asked to be fed and kept warm. One cold winter day, a sow had little piglets, and Dad brought them into the kitchen to keep them warm. It makes me wish we hadn't rigged up an old magneto with wires which we used to shock the pigs. We could be nasty little buggers at times!

Butchering was a normal and common event on the farm. This summary may make the rest of you join the family vegetarians, but these things were a reality on the farm, and we were hungry.

The only animals I did myself were the chickens. I would take the chosen one by both legs and both wings, take the ax in my other hand, lay the neck on a stump, and WHACK. Then we dipped the chicken in very hot water, plucked the feathers, gutted them, and they were ready for a roast, or we would cut them into halves or quarters for grilling.

Butchering pigs was a job for the big boys, like Tucker. Pigs were hard to kill. If they weren't too big or mean, Tucker would take a very sharp knife and slit their throat. Big or mean pigs would be shot with a rifle, then bled out. The intestines were removed, along with some organs like liver, which some people ate. The next step was to dip them in a large barrel of near boiling water, after which we used scrapers to remove the bristly hair from the skin. I can remember the smell of this step. It was not a bad smell, a little bit like burning wood though not nearly that strong. The pigs were then cut up into hams, slabs of bacon, pork loins and chops, etc. Pieces were carefully wrapped in paper and taken to our food lockers in Cazenovia or Canastota. The hams were cured under orange wooden barrels in our side yard. They would suspend the hams in the barrels, and burn corncobs in the bottom of the barrel to smoke the ham. It was good ham. That smoky smell is a fond memory of those times.

Butchering cows was a similar process, except that Tucker hit them in the head with a sledge hammer to kill them. Usually the cow would drop straight down, and that was it, but I remember once he hit a big old cow, and she took off for the road, then turned around and charged back for the barn. We all scattered. But when she got back to the barn, she dropped right near the spot where she was hit. One thing I remember about the beef was the canned meat. Ma would cut some of the less desirable pieces into cubes about one-two inches in size, put them in glass jars with water, salt, and other spices, and boil the meat. This meat would last for the season stored in the cellar, and tasted really good. (I am hazy on the details of how this meat was cooked. Maybe she cooked it before putting it in the jars. I just don't remember.)

When I was little, the horses were the primary work animals on the farm. Horses pulled the wagons and other machinery. Occasionally I would drive a team of horses pulling a hay wagon and a hay loader, but this was usually a job for a bigger stronger person. I remember leading a horse connected to a long rope which had a hay hook on the other end. The hook was jabbed into loose hay on the wagon, and then hoisted up into the hay mow, by a series of ropes, pulleys, and tracks. Later, when I was older, my job was to spread the hay around in the barn. When the hay hook full of hay got where we wanted it in the hay mow, we would holler "TRIPP - ER' and the loader would drop the hay by yanking the rope. Someone else would holler "WHOA" to the person leading the horse. All of a sudden, in about 1948-1950, everything became mechanized, tractors did all the work, and the horses had nothing to do. Dad bought an old school bus and cut the body off it. It made a pretty good hay wagon, and was my first vehicle to drive. I drove loads into the barn, which required a sharp turn, up a ramp, onto the barn floor, and a quick stop before the bus went out the back side of the barn. We loved our horses, and kept them around for a long time. About all we did with them was ride them bareback down to get the cows for milking. One last memory of the horses is that they could tell time. They would plod along at a slow, steady pace all through the day. Then along about 5:00 when we had to quit field work to go milk, they would know their day of work was over, and would head for the barn at a near gallop!

You all know what the bull was for, and so did we, even though Dad and Ma didn't want us to know too much. That is why they kicked us out of the barn when the bull was called upon to do his duty.

So we would leave the barn as requested, but would sneak up to one of the many windows and watch the entire process. Very educational. Talking about sex reminds me of another Aunt Mary story. When I was quite little, we were on our way to church. Dad, Ma, and Aunt Mary were in the front seat, and a bunch of us kids were in back. I said "Ma, what is sex?"

There was a brief silence, then Aunt Mary said, "You be quiet. We are on our way to church!" No wonder we peeked through the windows.

Flies were another "animal" of interest on the farm, but only because they were so thick and troublesome. They were so thick in the barn that you would sometimes have to hold your breath to keep from inhaling them. We sprayed often, but I would say not often enough. They were in the house by the hundreds. We had these fly stickers hanging from the ceiling, and it wasn't long after you put one up that they were black with buzzing flies. One of our indoor sports was swatting flies. If you recall the fable *Seven at a Blow,* that was nothing compared to what we could do. I do wonder why we didn't get more diseases, considering all the opportunities for things to happen. I think we developed a pretty high immunity.

There were a lot of snakes around the farm, but no poisonous snakes. Unfortunately, we used to hunt the snakes and usually killed them. Sometimes we would catch one and keep it, feeding it mice. One type of snake that often startled us was the spotted adder, which grew 4-6 feet long, and liked to crawl into the manger in front of the cows. We dispatched those very quickly.

The Crick

A beautiful stream, which we called "the crick" ran between our house and Pick's house. It started way up on the hills to the South and flowed down through a woods, over beds of shale, down through the pasture behind Pick's barn, through the tunnel under the road, wandered down through our pasture, and finally over a limestone ledge into our woods and beyond. We loved the crick, and we loved the tunnel.

The tunnel was about a four-foot diameter concrete culvert, where we spent a lot of time planning our next adventure, or hiding from the results of our last one. For instance, we sat in there for a while after Ma Keville spanked me with the butcher knife. We sat facing across the culvert, with the water running under our legs. I guess there couldn't have been too much water flowing if we could do that, but it seemed like a lot at the time.

There were nice little pools formed up where the water ran down over the shale. We often went swimming up there, without bathing suits, of course. We spent lots of time in the tunnel talking about how we could get the neighborhood girls up there in the same condition, but it never worked out!

Down in the pasture below our house, where it was pretty flat, the crick eroded out the stream banks. We would dig out the overhanging sod chunks, and build dams across the stream, where we would again go swimming. These dams would only last until the next big rain, but the real fun was in building them.

One time me and Bill and Pick and Dave decided to burn out woodchucks. We had learned that if you started a fire in one hole of a woodchuck den, that he would come out his other hole and you could hit him with a club. So we got some paper, a ball bat, and matches. The woodchuck den was down near Pick's, and he said that they had some kerosene we could use to get the fire going. This is where we got in trouble. The Pickards had two 55-gallon drums side by side on their porch, one filled with kerosene, which burns easily but is not real volatile, and the other filled with gasoline, which is highly volatile, as you will see. Of course, we got gasoline by mistake.

We marched out to the field with our supplies. Soon we had the hole stuffed with paper. Bill poured in the "kerosene," Pick and I guarded the exit hole, and Dave struck a match and dropped it in the hole. Nothing happened at first, but just as Bill and Dave looked down into the hole, BOOM, the thing exploded. Both of them had their hair singed, their eyes were watered, and they had an immediate sunburn.

We ran for the tunnel, and spent a while throwing water in their faces, and deciding what to do next. After a bit they started to hurt, and we decided we had to confess. We took them to our house, where Ma looked them over, applied a little ointment, and pronounced them cured. As usual, she was angry but nice. That was the end of burning out woodchucks. One thing we asked ourselves was, why would Stanley Pickard store a 55-gallon drum of gasoline on his porch? Not too bright.

Way up where the crick came onto Pick's land, there was a dump. You would be arrested if you dumped stuff there today, but back then there were little dumps everywhere. Anyway, we used to go up there, and each pick a favorite can, which we would put in the water and race all the way down into our woods, probably a mile or so. There were rules. You couldn't touch your can unless it was stuck, and then only after everybody else had passed you. This was fun and passed a lot of time. See why we didn't miss having Nintendo?

Another adventure involved that same dump. One day Stanley Pickard told Pick to go up and get the cows, which were in a high brush-covered pasture near the dump. Me and Bill and Dave said we would help get the cows. As we headed up along the crick, I had an idea. I suggested we go to the dump, get some bigger cans, put rocks in them, and sneak up on the cows. When we were close, I would give a signal, we would all jump up from behind the bushes, rattle our cans and shout, and watch what would happen. So we did just that. We spread out, crept carefully up to the cows, and on my signal, made a really infernal racket. Well, the result should have been obvious. From our vantage point up on the hill, we watched in awe as the cows stampeded down the hill in a cloud of dust, through the crick, into the barnyard, into the barn through an open door, and out the other end of the barn, through a door which may or may not have been open. The last we saw of the cows, they had crossed the road and were still running. I don't know how long it took Stanley to round up those cows, because Bill and I decided to take a very long detour to get home, and stayed out of Stanley's sight for a long time after that.

Fatty Mulligan was a nice guy but he was...fat. One beautiful, warm day Pick and I were laying around deciding what to do next. We wandered down into the pasture near the crick, and stood in the shade of the hedgerow which divided our property from Eddie Manwarren. There were some nice trees in the hedgerow, all overgrown with vines, which hid the tree and formed a canopy on top. Pick and I climbed up the vines, and laid down on the canopy of grapevines, watching the clouds roll by.

Along came Bill. He said "Mike and Pick, what are you doing up there, and can I come up?" I said "Well, I don't know if this tree will hold us all, but I guess you can come up." So up he came, and we all laid back and relaxed, watching the clouds roll by. Along came Dave. He wanted to join us. I thought he would be one too many, but Pick and Bill said OK, so up he came, and we all laid back and relaxed, watching the clouds roll by. Then along came Fatty Mulligan. Fatty said, " Hi, Bill and Mike and Pick and Dave." And we said, "Hi, Fatty." Fatty asked if he could come up, but we all shook our heads and I said, "No, Fatty, we have too many people here now." He was sad. Dave and Bill thought we should let him up, and Pick and I didn't want him to be sad, so we told him to come on up.

He huffed and puffed, and finally got to the top with the rest of us. However, just as we started to relax, the tree began to sway, and slowly, with a cracking of limbs, it tipped over and threw us all into the crick. Because it was a warm day, and because the tree tipped over slowly, no harm was done, we all had a good laugh, and we were happy that Fatty Mulligan did not go away sad and alone. [Author's note: this is the only story I tell which is not completely true. There is no Fatty Mulligan. Sorry. All the rest of the story is true. The four of us were in the top of a tree which tipped over and dumped us in the crick.]

Me 'n Bill 'n Pick 'n Dave

We did have a great time growing up in the neighborhood. We were good at thinking up things to do which were fun, even though some ideas got us in big trouble, as I have already described. There were other kids in the area, and lots of visitors, so we had a lot of the usual games like football and baseball. We weren't very good, but it was fun. We had little mercy when someone got hurt. We would drag them off the field and let them lay there moaning and groaning until we were sick of playing. If they still couldn't get up, we would then help them back to the house.

If nobody was around, I would get a stick, stand in our stony driveway, and hit stones as far as I could. I was a Dodgers fan, and could go right through the lineup as I hit them out there. Fun.

There was a round rock in our back yard. Sometimes we would each get a worm, place them in the center of the rock, and race them to see whose worm got to the edge of the rock first. Unfortunately, we got the idea of taking a magnifying glass, or just my eye glasses, and focus the sun's rays on the poor worms to move them along a little faster. It worked, too. We had similar races with snails, which were plentiful in the woods north of our house.

We spent a lot of time in the woods north of our house. There were deep woods, ravines, the crick with a few fish in it, and ledges of limestone with fossils imbedded. We spent a lot of time looking at those fossils, without realizing that the place where we were sitting must have been at the bottom of the sea in the long ago past. We would look for Indian arrowheads, and just sit around and talk, or lie on our backs and look up at the clouds. With our imaginations, we saw all kinds of animals.

There was a place down in the woods called Rattlesnakes Den, which was a big horseshoe shaped depression with cliffs on three sides, and heavily wooded. Many trees were tangled with vines, and we used to swing on the vines, out over the cliffs, and down into the valley below. We never did see any rattle snakes.

We often took a lunch with us, and sometimes cooked hotdogs. Once Dugan came with us and we started a hotdog fire in a little pit we arranged. We were sitting around the fire, when a stone which must have had some moisture trapped in it suddenly exploded. A hot piece of the rock flew inside Dugan's shirt, and burned him quite badly. We ripped off the shirt and threw water on him, but he was in pain and we hurried him home. I think that called for a trip to the Doc., and he still has the scar. Another bad game we used to play occurred in the same area where Dugan got burned. In the s p r i n g , when there was a lot of dead dry grass, we would split into teams of firebugs and firemen. The firebugs would go around setting fires in the dry grass, and the firemen would come around and put out the fires. We needed adult supervision!

Ma was pretty lenient with us, as long as we stayed on our own property or on Pick's or Dave's property, or sometimes Tucker's. This comprised 400 acres or more, so we had lots of room to roam. She did not want us to go all the way through the woods to the roads on the other side. One day we asked her if we could do just that, and she said NO. We agreed to stay in our own woods, packed a lunch, and were off. After a while, Dave suggested we go see Sonny Davis, who lived on a farm on the far side of the woods. We knew better, but agreed to go there, where we spent the rest of the day playing. By 4:30, we were very tired, and weren't looking forward to the long walk home. We decided to go home the long way, by road, but just as we started, in pulled Ma with the car. We were real glad to see her, as we were tired and needed a ride home. Our happiness didn't last long when she wouldn't let us get in the car, and made us walk all the way home in front of the car. When we got home, she told us to wait in the yard. She went in the house and got the razor strap, a leather belt used to sharpen shaving razors, and proceeded to give us a good whipping, which we deserved.

Needless to say, we never left our property without permission again.

One time, me 'n Bill 'n Pick 'n Dave were playing up in the hay barn. After a while, we sat up in an open door in the top of the barn to rest, Dave lost his balance, and fell about fifteen feet to the ground. He didn't get hurt, and Bill insisted that the reason why was that he, Bill, had thrown some hay out after Dave fell, and it got to the ground first and broke Dave's fall. Do you believe this story?

Another time, Dave told us he'd heard that if you grabbed a skunk by the tail and got his feet up off the ground, he wouldn't spray you. This sounded logical, so we set out to try it. Down in the woods behind Dave's house, we saw a skunk, and we crept slowly and carefully up to it through the weeds. Dave reached for the skunk's tail just as it arrived at its hole. He lifted it up, but the skunk's feet were in the hole, and Dave got a good spraying. What to do next?? Well, Dave took off all his clothes, and we trudged up to his house through the fields, not getting too close to Dave, for obvious reasons. When we got to his house, Aunt Jessie got a washtub, Dave sat in the tub, and she washed him down with tomato juice, followed by a hosing down with water. She was a gentle soul, and didn't bother to tell us how stupid we were, since we already knew.

In the winter, we went sliding downhill on all the big hills around our house. Some of the best sliding was in the road, since they didn't sand the road very often, and the traffic was light.

Sometimes we went farther from home than we should have. For example, once we went down a long hill leading away from the farm, leaving a very long uphill walk home. No sooner had we got to this far away location when I had to go to the bathroom real, real bad. I tried very hard to make it, but I am ashamed to admit that I was about half a mile short of making it home. I will not describe the gory details, but when I got home neither Ma nor I were very happy, although as I recall, Bill, Pick, and Dave got quite a charge out of it.

In the summer, we loved to go swimming. Sometimes, when we were older, Ma would take us to town after a hard day's work, and we would swim in the lake. We were dirty from working all day, and the townies didn't think much of us washing off in their lake. When we were young, we would swim in the crick after building a dam, or more often, we would swim in the small farm ponds scattered around the neighborhood. This sounds nice, except for the cows. We would be swimming in the dirty water at one end of the pond, while a bunch of cows were standing around in the other end polluting the local environment. Please tell me why we weren't all taken away by hideous disease!

Ma's Relatives

Ma was born in Cazenovia, well, really out in the hills between Nelson and Erieville. If you think Perryville was in the sticks, you should see where Ma spent her childhood, on Jackass hill. Her Father was Jim Ryan, a fine man whom I enjoyed when I was a kid. He died of cancer when I was about thirteen years old. He worked hard all his life. He was a farmer on some pretty poor soil on Jackass hill, then he was a custodian and grave digger for the church late in life. He wound up owning three or four houses in Cazenovia. I don't know where he got the money, as they were broke most of the time when the six children were growing up. Ma's Mother was Ellen Baker, who died in the flu pandemic of 1918-1920. Ma was about eleven years old at the time. The story is that she was feeling fine, they went to an anniversary celebration, she got sick the next day or so, and was gone within a very few days, leaving Grandpa Ryan with 6 kids, one of which, Aunt Peg (Fiedler), was a newborn. The oldest was Aunt Mary (Macaulay) about age thirteen, followed by Mom, Uncle Pat, Uncle Tom, and Aunt Jane (Goldacker).

They lived in a very isolated house up on a hill, far from most neighbors, and far from any work for Grandpa, except the poor farm they were running. I think they must have moved into town shortly after Grandma Baker Ryan's death. In any case, Grandpa could not care for all those children, so he gave Peggy and Jane to relatives who lived quite far away. In a year or two, Grandpa remarried to a woman named Kennedy. At the wedding, the people who had Jane presented her back to the family. So much for the honeymoon. That union resulted in one more child, Kaye (LeFevre). The Kennedy wife died after only a few years of marriage, and I think Kaye was farmed out to another family, who took real good care of her and eventually she stayed with them until she grew up. Grandpa eventually married again, to Margaret Burke, who died in about 1950. The Ryans did OK all through the depression, by each working hard and pooling their money to get by. Their real trouble started when they all got married and when WWII came along, which happened almost concurrently for many of them. Grandpa Ryan and all the wives, along with Tom, are buried in the Cazenovia cemetery.

Suzanne has written a better description of this time in the Ryan family, based on interviews with Ma and Jane Goldacker. The paragraphs below are by Suzanne. Thanks, Sue.

I would like to straighten out all these notes that I took from Gramma Anna in the '80s and ' 90s so this is a good time to do so! The oldest record that I have from her is that James Ryan married Bridget Hayes back in Ireland. They were from Tipperary in Ireland and are buried in the Cazenovia, NY, Saint James cemetery. They had a bunch of children, who were all born in Ireland: Margaret, Mary, Catherine, Bridget, Michael; and they must have all come to Central New York State.

Margaret Ryan, just mentioned, married Patrick Ryan (note that both Margaret and Patrick were named Ryan) who had been born in Ireland. He planned to go to Australia but when he sent money ahead to the Australian Ryans for a ticket, which was cheaper if purchased in Australia, those relatives spent the money and said they "had come upon hard times." So he said "forget Australia, I'll go to America." They came to America on the same boat, where they met, leaving from Liverpool, England. They had children named Mary (Durkin), Bridget (Purcell), Anna (Kelley), John Ryan and James Ryan. James married Ellen Elizabeth Baker, called Nellie, and they had Mary (Macaulay), Anna (Danehy), Patrick, Thomas, Jane (Goldacker) and Peggy (Fiedler). After Nellie died (around 1920) James Ryan married Kittie Kennedy and had one more child, Kaye (LeFevre).

Anna Danehy and Francis (Buster) Danehy were parents to William, Michael, Patricia (Hagan), James, and Mary Ellen Danehy.

Nellie Baker Ryan's parents were Thomas Baker, who lived to be about eighty, and Jane Boyle Baker, who lived to be about 100. Jane had come from Ireland at age nineteen and worked for the wealthy Ledyard family at Lorenzo in Cazenovia, as did her brother Matt. They saved money and sent it back to bring the other siblings to America. Nellie's siblings were Mary (Kelly), James, Leonard and Matthew. Nellie died when she was 38 in 1920.

James and Ellen Baker Ryan, circa 1900.

James Ryan and Nellie lived way up in the country outside of Erieville, NY on Holmes Road, over a hill called Jackass Hill by the locals. It was all they could afford, I suppose. James' parents were celebrating their 50 years of marriage and although it was wintertime James and Nellie headed out from their farm by horse and sleigh with their 6 children. The horses fell down numerous times getting through the snow. After Mass, they all went to Aunt Mary Durkin's house for the party, rolled up the rugs and danced away. One month later, Anna's mother (Nellie) died from complications of the flu. Gramma Anna called it Swine Flu, but now we think of it as Spanish Flu. First Patrick had it, then Mary, then momma Nellie and then Anna. The children were all on their mother's bed to visit and see her, and she cried and cried, knowing she was going to die. Gramma Anna was about 11 years old at the time. Her sister Peggy (about 8 months old) was sent to Bridget Purcell's (James Ryan's sister) and Jane (about 2 yrs old) went to Mary (Baker) Kelly's in Utica.

In April the family moved to Liberty Street in Cazenovia, NY. Meanwhile, Nellie's brother Matt (who later had a liking for alcohol) came to look after the children and Grampa Ryan arranged to sell the country property. After the move, Grampa went to work at a canning factory. Fresh green beans were delivered to the house, the family snapped the beans for canning, and the beans were collected the next morning. They did this so they could get electricity in the house. After the canning factory closed, he worked as a caretaker and then janitor at St. James Church.

A couple months after Nellie died, a telegram came for Grampa Ryan. Aunt Mary Durkin and Aunt Kate Ryan steamed it open and saw that Kitty (Kennedy) "proposed" to Grampa. Kitty had been Nellie's best friend. Two years later, Grandpa and Kitty were married. On their wedding day, Aunt Mary Kelly unexpectedly brought Jane, now age 4, home to live with her father and Kitty. Aunt Mary Durkin had come to help overnight , and when Grampa called to check on the children, he was informed that the Kelleys had brought Jane back to him, a big surprise on his wedding day! The Boyles, on the other hand, had a very hard time parting with Peggy.

Here is the story Aunt Jane and Gramma Anna told me on Thanksgiving day, 1992: When Kitty became pregnant with Kaye, it was discovered that Kitty had breast cancer, and in fact had a breast removed. She lived for 2 years after Kaye was born. When Kitty was ill Anna's sister Mary (Macaulay) age sixteen, quit school to take care of her, but Kitty's brother, Mike Kennedy, wanted to take care of her. After Kitty died, Mike sent a bill to Grampa Ryan for his services in caring for his own sister! That was in 1926. There was some insurance money Grampa had received after her death so Mike figured out this was the way to get it. It made Anna so angry (and her dad paid it) that she would not go to Mike Kennedy's wake or funeral, and her husband Buster never knew this until I was with them in 1984 at Vero Beach where we spent some time talking about family history. Truth be known, Anna didn't like Kitty and the feeling was mutual.

The Ryan siblings - Jane, Tom, Peg, Pat, Kaye, Mary, Anna, circa 1960.

Now Kaye had actually been named Sarah Theresa Ryan, and when her mother had become ill with cancer, Sarah was 2 and went to stay with Bridget and Pat Carroll in Syracuse, at Kitty's request. They called her Kaye and kept her at their house for a long time. At about age ten or twelve she was told that James Ryan was her real father and that she had brothers and sisters. When she found that out she was angry and confused. As a teenager she was a normal active girl and Bridget wasn't feeling well (cancer) so she sent Kaye back to be with the Ryan family. Kaye cried, but worse, Pat Carroll felt so terrible about her leaving that he went crying to Grampa Ryan that he couldn't live without her. So Grampa Ryan said the Carrolls could take her back if Kaye wanted to go, but it was permanent, not a back and forth situation. Kaye wanted to go back, though she had wonderful times with her half sisters, especially Jane and Peg, who were close to her age. That was the end of her confusion, though Aunt Peg started going to visit her and kept in touch. Grampa Ryan was very sorry he had given her back to the Carrolls, by the way. Kaye eventually changed her name officially to Katherine Carroll. Anyway, Bridget died while Kaye was still young, soon after her marriage to Joe LaFevre, but Pat lived to be almost 100.

After Kitty died Grampa married Margaret Burke. Peg and Jane were still young and liked to kneel down and say prayers with their father, tweaking his nose and kissing him goodnight, but after he married Margaret they couldn't do that and were jealous. James and Margaret were married about thirteen years. She died at about age fifty, but he lived until 1951, dying of bladder cancer at age 72. His later years were spent living with Aunt Peggy.

Thank you, Sue. Now back to Mike's narrative.

One little story about Grandpa Jim. When he was sick with cancer, but still getting around, he was out for a walk. We were at the Liberty Street house visiting. I was on the front porch, messing around as usual. I got up on the porch railing and jumped off onto the floor, knocking some furniture around and making a huge racket. Aunt Peg thought that Grandpa had fallen, and came charging out of the house. When she saw it was me, she gave me a swat and some choice words. I said nothing, but I did not think I had done anything wrong, and was very angry. I steered clear of Aunt Peg for several years after that. I had a terribly long memory for what I considered to be errors in judgment by adults.

Let's talk some more about Ma's relatives. They all lived around Cazenovia and we saw a lot of them, both in town and out at the farm, which they all loved and enjoyed visiting. Sometimes the whole family would meet at the farm for parties, and some, especially the Goldackers, would stay for a few days.

Aunt Mary Macaulay married Alex. They had 8 kids and lived in half a house in Cazenovia. Aunt Jane Goldacker, her husband Ernie, and their 6 kids lived in the other half. Neither family had much money, and times were tough for them for a long period. One good story about the Macaulays concerns food, which always seemed plentiful in that house, even though money was short. Now, I have told you that we were poor too, but eventually when Ma went to work and Dad got the farm going, we were doing OK. Anyway, one holiday, Macaulays invited us to join them for dinner. Since they were poor at the time, they had been given a lot of food by different organizations, including ham, turkey, and all the trimmings. There we were, 10 Macauleys and 7 Danehys, stuffing our faces and drinking beer, when the doorbell rang. It was another group passing out turkeys! Dad and Ma were quite embarrassed to be sponging off free food, but we did have a good laugh over the situation.

Eventually, Alex, who had injured his leg in a factory accident, was able to get a good job in Massena, NY, with General Motors. Most all of the Macaulay children graduated from college and all have led successful lives, but it wasn't easy at times.

Uncle Alex liked his beer. Once when we went to visit them in Massena, Alex asked me if I would like a beer. I said sure, so he brought out a quart, poured me a glass, and drank the quart while I drank the glass. We repeated this sequence through several quarts, and I was quite impressed with his consumption ability!

Jane Goldacker and Ernie had it tough. Ernie was an electrician, but after returning from the navy in WWII, where he was on a repair ship for about 3 years, he did not work a steady job. I have never discussed it with his children, but I wonder if he wasn't affected more than the other relatives by the war. Back then, nobody gave a second thought to the traumatic effects of war.. Who knows what he went through? Anyway, that family, too, grew up and most of them are still living in or near Cazenovia.

Tom Ryan was a great guy. He never married. He worked as a pipe coverer for an asbestos firm. He was one of the only members of the union to get retirement benefits. Virtually all the rest of his coworkers died of lung cancer from breathing in asbestos fibers. He loved all his nephews and nieces. Sometimes when he would come to visit, he would reach out to shake hands with us, and sometimes, especially when we were in college, he would have a twenty-dollar bill concealed in his hand. We were supposed to just stick it in our pocket and not make a fuss, which we did. Tom owned the house that the Macaulays and Goldackers lived in. Tom was in the 14th Armored division during WWII. He had some rough times, including being bitten by a spider while training, which nearly finished his military career before it started. He saw some serious action but never talked much about it. I remember that he was very emotional on Memorial Day. He would cry, and when the guns were fired as part of the ceremony, he would shake like a leaf. In later life, he lived with Emma Michel and, unfortunately, her mother, who ruled the roost. Tom told cousin Ed more than Ed wanted to know about that relationship. The bottom line was that it was not a romance made in heaven.

Pat Ryan married Rose Long, and they had three children. Pat went to business school. He was in the army in WWII, but I don't think he suffered the trauma that the others did. I believe he was in England most of the time, but he did his duty and was proud of his army time. After the war Pat worked for the local electric company, and then Niagara Mohawk Power Co., where he had quite a good job. Pat believed in living on "the top shelf" as much as possible, although always within his means. He loved that phrase, and sometimes we called him "top shelf" behind his back. It was fun to see Pat and Rose, and they were almost always present at family parties.

Margaret "Peg" married Harold "Butch" Fiedler during the war, and they had two children, Frances and Ed. We spent a lot of time with Peg and Butch. Their house was always available to us late at night when we were waiting for a ride home from town. I babysat the Fiedler kids, with the usual stipulation regarding diapers. They always had Joan Goldacker stay too, to feed me and the kids and do the dirty work.

Butch was in the Army Air Corps in WWII. He trained as a radio man on a bomber, but during training, his plane crashed and he was injured, knocking out his teeth and other damage as well. He and Peg had planned to be married after his training, but he felt so bad about his damaged face that he wanted to postpone marriage. Peg would have none of that, and went down to his duty station in the Carolinas, where they got married. After that, he was taken off flight status, and was eventually sent to the jungles of Burma, where he worked on communications with bombers in the war in the Pacific. He never got home until 1946.

Butch has always been a proud Mason, having been raised in the Masonic Orphanage in Utica, NY. He is proud of the fact that his gravestone in the Catholic cemetery in Cazenovia has the only Masonic emblem in the whole place.

When Sue and I were having our pre-marriage counseling, the priest asked us what married couple most represented the kind of marriage we would like to have, we both agreed that Peg and Butch were that couple. While all the people mentioned in this document had long marriages, I can tell you first hand that none of them were more admirable as married couples than Peg and Butch, and many of the others fell well short of the standard set by Peg and Butch. As an aside, that same priest, Father Gorman, told Sue and I another fact of life. He said "there is only room for one boss in a family, and that's you." and he pointed to one of us. You will have to guess who he pointed to!

Kaye LeFevre was Ma's half sister. She didn't live in Caz, and I didn't know her much at all, though I have met her a few times in later years. She is a very nice person, and looks a lot like Aunt Jane used to look. She and her family live in the Detroit area.

Matt Baker was Ma's uncle. He was a bachelor who "liked the drink," as the Irish used to say. He was a bit of a loner, and didn't stay in any one place for too long of a time. I mention him because he lived with us on the farm for quite a while. He was one of many who Dad and Mom took in at one time or another. He was a good worker when he was sober, so it wasn't all charity. He helped with the cows, and helped clean the house and do kitchen work. However, we kids weren't known for our compassion, and weren't always nice to Uncle Matt. In fact, we drove him crazy, would never do what he said, and eventually he got sick of us and left, walking the ten miles back to Cazenovia. Boy, we could be nasty buggers.

World War II

I only have a few memories of WWII. I remember admiring, and I still admire, all the men from the Ryan family who went to war. Ernie, Tom, Butch and Pat really did their duty. It must have been very tough on all the families, and it is miraculous that they all returned safely. The Danehy people were mostly farmers, and as such were exempt from military service.

I remember ration books. You had books full of coupons, which you traded in when buying rationed items, like gasoline, tires, sugar, butter, and other items. I remember air raid drills, with blackout curtains and lamps with tiny bulbs in the base to give a little light. I remember going with Dad to spot airplanes. We went to a little shack up on a hill near Clockville, where we sat and looked for airplanes going over. We had silhouettes of all the German planes to help in identification. I don't think we saw any planes when we were on duty. I remember going out to pick up milkweeds, for use in making parachutes. And lastly, I remember a B-17 bomber which crashed a few miles away. I don't remember what happened to the crew.

I vaguely remember the end of the war in August 1945. I wish I had a stronger memory of the great joy they all must have felt to have the war end. It seems odd that I have such a clear memory of the day President Roosevelt died, but no clear memory of the end of the war.

92

Suzanne

I didn't have too much luck with the ladies when I was in high school, but not for lack of trying. For one thing, I was six feet one, 145 pounds, and not very coordinated. One of Sue's memories of me was at assemblies, when I would sometimes be lucky enough to be called up on stage to receive a prize or certificate. She says I looked all arms and legs, flailing away to get up there and back to my seat without falling down. I did know a lot of girls, and they were mostly nice to me, but I think they considered me harmless.

A few examples may help. Once I got a date with a nice girl named Maryann Schiltz. I picked her up in Bill's car, and unfortunately Bill came with it. So Maryann was in the front seat in the middle, I was driving, and Bill was sitting by the window. Before we had gone two blocks, Bill and I got in an argument, and he hauled back and threw a punch right across Maryann's face and hit me in the jaw. She was so frightened that she jumped over the seat into the back. I slammed on the brakes, we jumped out and had a fight, and I don't remember much else about the evening. I do remember that was my first and last date with Maryann Schiltz.

Another time I took Myrna Estey to the movies. We were in the back seat of the car on the way home when I got up my nerve to try for a kiss. I put my arm around her, closed my eyes, leaned in, and proceeded to kiss my shirt collar which was sticking up between us. End of romantic episode. Another time I came home from college, called Myrna and asked her to go out on a date. She said "Gee, I'd like to, but I'm married." That ended my romancing of Myrna Estey.

Yet again, I took a beautiful girl, Anne Smith, to the junior prom. Everything went well until I brought her home at 6:00 am, which apparently her father thought was a little late, since he came charging out of the house when I pulled up in front. I pushed her out of the car and took off before he got to the road, but that was the last date with Anne Smith.

Another problem I had with the girls may have been due to the guys I hung around with, and the tricks we played. One night a bunch of us went to Ellen Flanagan's house. She was a great person, and a lot of fun in a group. We made ourselves at home. Her father smoked pipes, and had a nice collection. He also had a sword collection. Before long, we were smoking his pipes, and sparring with his swords. Unfortunately Mr. Flanagan came home while we were enjoying his prized possessions. He was not too pleased and we left very soon thereafter. I don't think Ellen had a high opinion of us after that.

Another time, Noretta Spaulding was babysitting for Jiggs Ryan's kids and we decided to pay her a visit. After a while, when Noretta and some of our group were in the living room, my friend Ted Clarke (one of Sue's old boyfriends, by the way) and I went out to the kitchen. He laid down on the floor and I poured catsup on his chest, and placed a catsup covered knife nearby. We then started arguing and he shouted "don't, don't" and we thumped on the floor. She came running out, took one look, and screamed bloody murder. To say she was mad would be an understatement, and we left very soon thereafter. Maybe there was a reason the girls didn't take me seriously.

But then in the summer of 1957, my luck changed. For a long time I had admired this girl who was two years behind me in school. Our families had known each other forever, and she had been at the farm a few times when Dad and Ma hosted the Knights of Columbus picnic. She hung around with some of the same gang I did, but mostly I admired her from afar. Actually my brother Bill took her out before I did, but that didn't last more than one date. Anyway, Bill and I used to have a big clam bake in the orchard below our house every summer, and I invited Suzanne to come to the party. This was a big blowout every year, with three barrels of beer, three bushels of clams, hotdogs, corn on cob, etc., lots of music, and a huge bonfire. We charged ten dollars for each male who attended, but ladies were free. We had money collectors and bouncers to see that everyone paid. This group agreed not to drink until all had paid or were ushered to the road. The party went on all night. One year it rained and we all went in the house. Ma, why did you put up with us? Anyway, Sue said she would come, but I think she was a little shocked at all the action. She was also shocked that I drank about 15 beers that night. She was very impressed at how much attention I paid to her through the evening, thinking what a nice host I was. Little did she know I had been waiting all summer to get up the nerve to ask her out. At the end of the evening (almost morning), I asked her to go to the movies the next night. She said yes, but thought I would never remember asking her, or would be too tired to go, or both.

But I arrived on her doorstep bright eyed and bushy tailed the next evening. Her sister Cathy answered the door, and much to Sue's embarrassment, immediately asked me "are you going to marry my sister?" Sue's mom told me that Cathy always asked Sue's dates that question and they were all trying to marry her off, so I should pay no attention. I will say that before very long I started having similar thoughts on my own. I still remember the movies we saw that night, a big double feature including Old Yeller and Gunfight at the OK Corral. I won't get

Suzanne Esther DeLorme, circa 1955.

into too much sex in this story, but I will say that she let me put my arm around her that night, and it wasn't too many dates before I was getting the occasional kiss goodnight.

We went out every possible night from then on until the day we married almost three years later. Dorothy DeLorme was worried that we were seeing too much of each other and told Sue we could only go out two nights a week. When I heard that, I was pretty angry, but Sue got her brother Paul and his girlfriend to convince Dorothy that two nights was not going to work, and that crisis was averted.

I hung out at the DeLorme house quite a bit during those years. They were very good to me, and Dorothy was a good cook so I took every advantage of that. One Thanksgiving I was there. Dorothy put on a delicious meal, and afterward, I helped Sue wash dishes. Sue asked me to take out the garbage, which I did and when I got back to the kitchen, I gave her a friendly pinch on the behind. The only problem was that while I was gone she and her mother had switched places, and it was her mother who I pinched! I was *very* embarrassed, and hid out for the rest of the day, hoping she would forget.

Dan DeLorme, on the other hand, was a poor cook. He was a carpenter, and hired me to work with him at times. I would stay over at their house and ride to work with him. He volunteered to cook my breakfast one day, soft boiled eggs. He cooked them and set two on my plate. When I cracked the shells, they ran all over the

The DeLorme family, circa 1952.

plate and onto the table. I never wanted to look at a soft boiled egg again. Dan was a talented builder, but not much of a cook, and not a good speller. One day he knew Sue and I were going to stop in, but he and Dorothy had to go away, so he wrote us a note. It said:

"Dear Sue and Mike, If you hunger, have a hambug."

Dan and Sue's sister Cathy had a wonderful relationship. Cathy came along at a time when they may have been looking forward to a little peace and quiet, but that didn't happen. Cathy was sick with asthma as a young child, and needed a lot of attention. A big turning point came when Dan bought her a horse. They had a great time with that horse, and at about the same time, Cathy went from being a little sickly to being a robust, enthusiastic teenager. I remember one time her mother was mad at her for going swimming in a nearby pond only days after the ice went out.

We had a big laugh at Dan's expense one night when we all went to the movies. He was a very regular church goer, but went to movies on rare occasions. That probably explains why he genuflected when he got ready to go to his seat at the movie. We howled with laughter, and he laughed too. He was a good sport.

Dan got a job doing some major repairs at the old St. James church in Cazenovia. My brother Jim worked on that job and tells this story. Dan had a guy named Don Haley working for him. Don was a real religious man, and each time he crossed in front of the alter, even if he was carrying an armload of lumber, he would kneel and bless himself. Dan let this go a few times, but eventually said, "damn it, Don, quit your damn genuflecting and get to work."

Dan wore himself out working on the houses he built. He didn't do well financially until right near the end of his working life, when he bought some good land in Cazenovia, built houses on the lots, and wound up with enough money to live a comfortable, if careful, older age. By the mid sixties, he was pretty worn out. Once they came to visit us in Canton, at a time when I was planning to redo our old 1920's kitchen. Dan was crawling around, stiff and sore, until he realized I couldn't figure out how to design the kitchen in an efficient layout. We sat down with him, and in short order he had a solution to our problems. He became very excited, made a list of materials, hurried me down to the lumber company, and helped rebuild the kitchen for the next few days. His aches and pains were forgotten.

I almost never rode with Dan in a car, because he drove in the middle of the road. But one day, I did ride uptown with him. This was when he was quite old and had cancer. We stopped at the traffic signal, and an old man started hobbling across in front of us. Dan said "watch this" and laid on the horn. The guy threw his cane and nearly collapsed, but Dan thought it was pretty funny.

Another time Sue took him uptown and he hobbled into the drugstore with her. She went to the pharmacy in back, and he stayed up front near the magazines. When she came back to the front of the store, he was happily reading Playboy magazine.

Cornell

I went to Cornell University in Ithaca, NY, beginning in 1955 and finishing in 1960. It was a five-year program in Agricultural Engineering. I earned 191 credit hours for a bachelor's degree. It should have been worth a master's, but wasn't! In fact, sometime in the '80s I wrote them a letter asking them to send me a master's diploma, since they had by that time dropped back to four years for the bachelor's degree. They said no, but eventually sent me a certificate saying that the degree I earned was equivalent to a masters.

Tuition was free in Ag. Engineering at that time, and I lived in a rooming house for seven dollars a week and worked for my meals, so I got along pretty well financially with some help from Ma and Dad.

At Cornell, as at most colleges, you stood in line a lot to register, especially as freshmen. So I went from one line to another, gradually making progress. I joined one long line, finally got to the front, and was surprised to see a man in military uniform. I stepped up, and he said, "Army or Air Force?"

I said "WHAT?...I don't know what you are asking.!" He told me that Cornell was a land grant university, and that every male student had to take two years of military training. I was totally surprised by this information, and mumble, "Army." After two years, I elected to take advanced training and get a U.S. Army commission as a second Lieutenant, mostly because it paid $29.00 per month. This story is important because it shows how a quick, poorly informed decision can affect your future. I did not like the army, but in the end it was very good for me.

I have always had mixed feelings about my Cornell experience. After I left, I had no desire to ever see the place again, until daughter Patsy went there. I read somewhere that trying to get an Engineering education at Cornell in the '50s was like trying to take a drink out of a fire hose, and that is pretty close to the truth. Even though Ithaca is in the beautiful Finger Lakes area of New York State, I was never able to enjoy the many parks because of academic demands. I was a very motivated student, largely because I knew I didn't want to go back to the farm and shovel manure the rest of my life. On the first day of orientation, there were fifteen of us Agricultural Engineering majors. On graduation day, there were two of the fifteen left. The rest fell by the wayside. However, it was not all work, mostly thanks to the fraternity, Alpha Gamma Rho, and a couple of classmates, Dave Sawyer and Ron Reeve.

Dave Sawyer was also an AGR, and a really good friend. He was very bright, but lazy. He would always find out how much the labs counted, and if they did not count more than 40% of the grade, he wouldn't do them, since 60% was passing, and he would plan to get a perfect score in the tests to get a passing grade. His system only broke down once, when a nasty professor only left room for the final answer to a very complicated problem, and Dave made a math error, wrote in the wrong number on the final, and failed the course. I remember that professor well. He marched into class on the first day and said "my name is Ruoff, and I'm from Purdue." I guess he thought we would all be pretty impressed with that, but we weren't. More impressive was the fact that he failed nearly half the class of junior engineering students. The sad thing is, he was a pretty good teacher, with a lot of good information, but gave tests you couldn't pass.

Another professor in Electrical Engineering told the class of several hundred students on the first day that "if there is anybody out there who thinks you can get over 60% on my tests, come down here and teach the course!" That certainly left everyone in a positive state of mind.

Well, back to Dave Sawyer, and a little about Ron Reeve. Ron and I were very competitive, and not just in class. The three of us walked together from class to class, often a long walk at Cornell. Ron and I would get in an argument, followed by pushing and shoving, and often followed by a wrestling match in the snow, mud, or rain. Dave would hold our books and tell us what fools we were, and he was right, except it did let us blow off steam.

Dave was a big clumsy farm boy from up on Seneca Lake. We always laughed at his walk, saying he looked like he was walking on plowed ground. He was the smartest person I knew at Cornell. When we were seniors, we would be working on a problem, and he would say "don't you remember freshman year when the Physics professor told us how to do this problem?" This from a guy who never took any notes in class. Dave stayed in school after I left, getting a masters in Engineering Physics, the hardest program at Cornell, and going to work for General Electric, working on transistors before they were called transistors. He eventually quit and went home to the farm. The sad end to this story is that Dave, always a little careless, ran out of gas on a tractor. He went back to the barn and got a can of gas, which he put on the seat next to him in the truck. The gas spilled, exploded, and he burned to death. Really a sad story.

The first two years at Cornell I worked at Delta Chi fraternity, a bunch of rich snobs who couldn't wait on themselves. They employed 12 of us to serve their meals and wash dishes. In return, we got all our meals. We had a lot of laughs there, mostly at their expense.

My brother Bill worked there, too, and once the menu was spaghetti and meatballs. The kitchen was in the cellar, along with the cook's sleeping quarters, and Bill's job was to take the large flat trays of meatballs out of the oven and carry them upstairs where we dished out the food onto plates before carrying the plates to the dining room. Anyway, Bill stumbled, and meatballs rolled under the stove, down the hallway, and into the cook's bedroom where some wound up under the bed.

Well, what would you do? Right. We quickly gathered up all the meatballs, threw them in the pot of sauce, and dished them out to the hungry brothers of Delta Chi where they hogged them down with their usual enthusiasm.

Delta Chi had a few obnoxious people who treated us poorly. One was named Oogie. Delta Chi had a rule that if someone was more than 5 minutes late for dinner, we didn't have to serve him. Oogie was very late one night, and demanded food in a loud and nasty voice. We were clearing plates, and spaghetti was again the main course. We told him it was too late, but he told us to get out there and get him some food! Again, what would you do? Right again!! We went to the garbage can, and carefully dished Oogie a nice big plate of spaghetti from the brothers leftovers. He didn't thank us, but he enjoyed his meal and so did we!

After the first two years, I got a job as a lab assistant in Agricultural Engineering, and joined advanced ROTC, which paid $29 a month. These were better jobs, but not as much fun as working at Delta Chi.

I had a lot of fun at AGR, and still have some friends from there, especially Max Fisher from Madrid, NY, who recently passed away. Late at night, I would go over to the house for coffee, toast, and conversation. There were always people sitting around shooting the bull about the usual topics (women, the last party, the next party). I lived in the house only one year, my junior year. It was too noisy and not conducive to good study habits, which I needed if I wanted to stay in school. Everyone slept in a big dormitory room on the third floor, in bunk beds. All the windows were left open all winter, and everyone slept in sleeping bags. I didn't wash mine all winter, and by the way that place smelled, no one else did either. One fall day, one of the guys shot a deer and hung it up in a tree in the yard. We didn't think that was proper, so we took the deer and put it nicely tucked in to the hunter's sleeping bag. Everyone thought this was hilarious except the guy who shot the deer! We were a typical obnoxious fraternity. Unfortunately, we played loud music, and since drinking wasn't allowed in the house, we had loud parties in the yard, which drew occasional visits from the cops. Many of the brothers had cars, some of which barely ran. I remember when several people wanted to go to an away football game at

Brown University. They had to jack up two or three cars in order to get enough good tires to get there and back. Another time, we built a jump in the yard, and drivers would come down the street, into the driveway, and see how far they could jump their car before disappearing down over an embankment on the back side of the property. On other occasions, people would fire shotguns out the windows of the house, trying to hit rabbits running across the lawn. A few brothers were just "no account." I remember two guys (can't remember their names) who got sick of school in the middle of the semester and decided to head West. They had an auction in the fraternity living room and sold everything they owned to finance the trip. They got a grand total of about fifty dollars for their possessions, and away they went!

We had a thing called criticism sessions once or twice a year. Small groups were formed, and the brothers proceeded to criticize one another. I guess this was a good idea in theory, but I didn't like it much. I mostly got criticized for not being around the house much, but that was necessary for me. One guy, Ferguson, really got nailed at a session for being a tightwad. He had a car, and would take a bunch of people to a bar. They would take turns buying drinks, but when it came Fergy's turn to buy, he would say it was time to go home. This happened several times, and eventually they showed no mercy in a criticism session, bringing him to tears. Some people had bad table manners, and their habits were a common discussion item at ths sessions. One guy, Goody, did

Sue and Mike at AGR pinning ceremony, circa 1958.

not learn his lesson at the session, so he suffered the consequences. His habit was that he would hog food at the table. We served family style, with about 8 people at each table. Goody would take most if not all of a dish of meat or veggies, not concerned about others. Soo...one night we had mashed potatoes, and Goody took well more than his share. People said "give Goody more potatoes." We passed the potatoes from all the tables to Goody, and people dished them onto his plate until there was a huge mound falling over onto the table, onto his lap, and onto the floor. Goody got the hint, and I suspect it was a lesson he remembered.

My Cornell experience would be incomplete without mentioning Suzanne. Although I knew her since we were young children, we didn't date until just before the start of my junior year. Look elsewhere in this saga for more details of this romance, but anyway, Sue came to Cornell for a few party weekends, and we had a very good time there. Because she didn't drink, and most of my fraternity brothers were intent on seeing how much they could hold, we didn't spend too much time at the parties, but we found other things to occupy our time. Once my Dad let her tdrive his '55 Oldsmobile to Ithaca for a party, which worked out nicely except for the fact that she didn't know how to get to Ithaca. Apparently, not trusting her map skills, she stopped at every four-corners between Cazenovia and Ithaca to ask directions. Anyway, she arrived safely and a good time was had by all. Once she stayed in a home where I rented a room. The rental rooms were on the third floor, and the Whitmans, the elderly couple who owned the house, lived on the first two floors. They generously allowed Sue to sleep in a spare bedroom on the second floor, near their own bedroom. Sue got up in the night to use the bathroom, and who did she run into in the hallway but a very fleshy Mr Whitman, heading back to bed from the same chore, and dressed only in a stocking cap. Sue says she didn't see a thing because she wasn't wearing her glasses, but I wonder.

I did not have transportation as a student, so it was a little difficult to see Sue as often as I would have liked. I hitchhiked up to Syracuse to see her when I could. This usually worked out very well. Some people would even go out of their way to take me all the way, or to take me to where it was easy to get another ride. I would wait until I got in the car before I would say where I was headed, so that if they looked suspicious, I could say I was just going down the road a mile or so, and then get out of the car. My only bad experience happened before I even left Ithaca, when a car driven by a grad student hit me just as I was ready to step off the sidewalk. I did a roll, landed on my feet, and was unhurt, but knocked off his rearview mirror. Us farm boys were tough.

One weekend in the Spring, I knew I had to stay in Ithaca to study. I wrote Sue and told her I couldn't come to Syracuse. By the way, I don't think we talked on the phone more than once or twice in all the years we dated. Long distance calls were too expensive. Anyway, I was in my room studying on Saturday morning when the mail came, with a letter from Sue. She said

Suzanne DeLorme Danehy and Michael Joseph Danehy on their wedding day, June 25, 1960, with their parents.

she was busy too, and in fact had made a plan to study all day Saturday in the library with her friend, Alan. Now I was a young man in love, and that letter didn't sound too good to me. I don't think I even finished the letter. I grabbed my sweater, and headed for the road with my thumb out. Two hours later I was in Syracuse, at the library. I saw her sitting with Alan, and casually sat down across from them and said hello. Sue started laughing, a little nervously I thought, but soon they finished their work and we went off to have a nice lunch. I know that was a little possessive, but it shows how much Sue meant to me.

Anyway, I finally graduated in June, 1960, we got married the next week, and I was working for Firestone Tire and Rubber Company by July 1, 1960.

And that is how I grew up on the farm.

About the Author

This whole book has been about the author. 'Nuff said.

Mike and Sue Danehy, still cruising, circa 2014.

www.ingramcontent.com/pod-product-compliance
Lightning Source LLC
Chambersburg PA
CBHW071639050426
42443CB00026B/751